Church Bells at Midnight

Church Bells at Midnight

A Church, its Neighborhood, and a Serial Killer

MATT HORAN

Foreword by Bob Buckhorn

RESOURCE *Publications* • Eugene, Oregon

CHURCH BELLS AT MIDNIGHT
A Church, its Neighborhood, and a Serial Killer

Resource Publications
An Imprint of Wipf and Stock Publishers
199 W. 8th Ave., Suite 3
Eugene, OR 97401

www.wipfandstock.com

PAPERBACK ISBN: 978-1-6667-1267-4
HARDCOVER ISBN: 978-1-6667-1268-1
EBOOK ISBN: 978-1-6667-1269-8

06/25/21

For Benjamin, Monica, Anthony, and Ronald
The hole left by the loss of these four extraordinary people in the lives of their families, friends, and neighbors can never be filled. By sharing this story, however, I hope the effect of their lives and deaths, and the powerful lessons learned by the church where I served and the neighborhood where we all lived, will be preserved and passed on for generations to come.

For Susan
You saw things in me I didn't know were there, helped me become someone I never thought I could be, and made a life with me even better than I knew I could hope for.

With Special Thanks to Sarah Ellis
For being brave, for being kind, for believing in my belief in you, and for being such a gift to the Horan family, and for April Fools Days.

Contents

Foreword

FOR 51 DAYS TAMPA stared into the abyss as a serial killer targeted four innocent victims in the Seminole Heights neighborhood of our city. Yet out of the darkness a neighborhood and the people who lived there refused to let evil win. They stood up in the face of fear, took care of each other and the police officers that protected them. It is a story of sadness, yes, but also of humanity, resilience, and the kindness of people like Rev. Matt Horan and the Seminole Heights United Methodist Church.

Bob Buckhorn
Mayor of Tampa
(2011–2019)

— Prologue —

We Are Seminole Heights

I'VE NEVER LIVED IN a neighborhood that had a logo before. Seminole Heights has two, and they're everywhere.

The first has been around for almost a century. It's got a two-headed alligator on it that comes from a Depression-era fable about such a beast roaming the banks of the Hillsborough River, which borders Seminole Heights.

The legend got new traction when a resident claimed to have snapped a photo of a two-headed alligator on the banks of the river in 2014, and to this day the owners and regulars of *Ella's Americana Folkart Cafe* claim that they have that same alligator preserved by a taxidermist and displayed proudly for anyone to see. While there's some debate about the details of the story, it had enough legs—the usual four, anyway—to give the old logo new life and appear on flags prominently displayed on the front porches of just about every street in the area.

You can find the other one everywhere too. It's newer, reflecting the unusually proud spirit of the neighborhood. A simple, circular emblem announces what you feel soon after you move in: *We Are Seminole Heights.*

The Seminole Heights neighborhood, just north of downtown Tampa, sprang up pretty fast after the turn of the twentieth century. As more people were needed to work at the Tampa Electric Company, the Plant Hotel (now the University of Tampa), and other employers in Tampa's increasingly bustling downtown area; a streetcar line was built running north from downtown up the middle of Central Avenue, a centrally located road into Seminole Heights. With transportation to downtown now easily accessible, Seminole Heights was a natural place for workers to live.

From the start, great care was taken to make the neighborhood a beautiful place. Designers of Seminole Heights' Hillsborough High School modeled it after buildings at the University of Notre Dame. It is still one of the most beautiful high schools in the country, with an auditorium featuring stained glass windows that give the room a cathedral-like feel.

Builders created a collection of bungalow style houses on a grid of cobblestone streets bordered by the Hillsborough River to the north and west, Martin Luther King Jr. Boulevard (MLK) to the south, and 22nd Street to the east. Almost every house was designed with a front porch, a carport, a crawl space underneath, and an alley behind it. You could usually see the front door from the back of the house, allowing breeze to flow through the house in the days before air conditioning.

The 1960s expansion of busy east-west streets such as MLK and Hillsborough Avenue, as well as the construction of Interstate 275 through the middle of Seminole Heights, separated different sections of the neighborhood, but a sense of pride and community still remains among residents. People sit on front porches, walk their dogs, and know their neighbors. They shop local and support each other's business ventures. A chain business in Seminole Heights is a rare find.

For example, as a prank in 2015 someone put a "Coming Soon: World of Beer" sign in a vacant lot near *Cappy's Pizza* and *The Independent*, two iconic restaurants in the neighborhood. The *World of Beer* location to the north near the University of South Florida was besieged by calls from residents complaining about their chain restaurant moving in. After answering the calls all day and trying to explain that there was no plan to open a location there, World of Beer took to their social media accounts to spread the word that they didn't put up the sign. It's not a prank that would work in most places, but whomever put that sign there knew it surely would in Seminole Heights.

Many of the original families moved farther out toward more suburban areas after crime, drug abuse, and prostitution began edging into the neighborhood during the 1980s and 1990s, causing a downturn in property values. Several of the bungalows became rental units, whose residents didn't take as much pride in how the neighborhood looked. A few small, unattractive used car dealerships popped up along the busiest north-south street in the neighborhood, Florida Avenue. The cool restaurants and shops on Florida became next door neighbors to parking lots full of cars in various stages of disrepair, some even with mistreated guard dogs barking at passers-by. Interstate-275 made the Central Avenue streetcar line unnecessary, so while the rails are still there nestled into the original cobblestone roads, they're now paved over, as are all but a few of the original cobblestone streets.

However, in the late 1990s and early 2000s, the area of Seminole Heights north of Hillsborough Boulevard became a trendy place. People fell in love with repurposing the old things that showed up in antique shops or estate sales. The pioneers of Seminole Heights passed away, leaving their homes to kids who had moved out of the area long ago. In many cases, these houses were put on the market by heirs eager to sell and close the book on their connection to the area. Good deals were there for the taking.

The mid-2000s housing boom bloated the formerly low prices overnight, and something of a land-rush took hold until 2008, when the housing market crashed. Many owners owed more money on the houses than they were worth. House flippers became landlords against their will, while others were forced to keep houses that they'd intended to fix up and resell, because even the fixed-up version wasn't a good return on their investment. Renewal was still on the horizon, but it was delayed.

By the mid to late 2010s, the delay was over. Finding an affordable house in Seminole Heights was like looking for the Loch Ness Monster—occasionally, someone would catch a glimpse of something, but it would either be a mirage, or it vanished before you could take a second look. Even tiny two-bedroom homes that needed a ton of work were being listed for $300,000 or more.

By 2017, the hunt for the elusive Seminole Heights home spilled out of the northern section. Yards were cleaned up, curb appeal was addressed, and remodeling projects were underway all over the place. A sense of pride seemed to spread to all corners of Seminole Heights. Residents were getting to know their neighbors, even calling each other's dogs by name while out on a walk. They were forming homeowners' associations, lobbying for infrastructure improvements, and using social media to beat the drum for supporting local businesses.

The corner of Frierson and N 15th is south of Hillsborough Avenue. The area around it is a relative latecomer to the neighborhood's restoration, but by 2017 it was underway. People near the intersection knew each other, looked out for one another, and felt a sense of community. They beat back crime by forming neighborhood watch groups, installing camera-doorbells, networking with each other on social media through *Facebook* and *Nextdoor*, and speaking up whenever something was amiss.

All of this is part of what made the Seminole Heights serial killer such a strange phenomenon. A man took out a gun, committed a murder, and vanished into the night. How could this have happened? Moreover, how did he get away with it a second time, then a third, and then a fourth? It baffled the police, infuriated the mayor, and terrified the people of Seminole Heights.

Unfortunately for Howell Emmanuel "Trai" Donaldson III, it had a galvanizing effect on just about everybody who lived in the neighborhood he chose for his killing spree. They were all in it together, and proud to wear the t-shirts, fly the flags, or just say it out loud: *We are Seminole Heights.*

In 2017, I was the pastor at Seminole Heights United Methodist Church. However, for those 51 days that year, I was just proud to *be* Seminole Heights.

The Murder of Benjamin Mitchell

Twenty-two-year-old Benjamin Edward Mitchell was a student at Hillsborough Community College. An aspiring musician, he booked a few gigs, worked at IKEA, and attended classes when he wasn't working. He kept a full schedule, but with no responsibilities on the night of October 9th, he left his house just before 9 p.m. He walked north two blocks and crossed the street to get to the bus stop on the corner of N 15th and Frierson. He was going to catch the route 9 bus and take it to visit his girlfriend.

N 15th Street has only two-lanes, but is fairly busy. It was the road I used to drive a carpool of kids from Seminole Heights to Orange Grove Middle School every morning. Sometimes I'd see the route 9 bus coming down Hillsborough to turn down 15th in the morning, and I knew that if I got ahead of it, I'd make great time. If it snuck in ahead of me somehow, I would be stuck behind it all the way down 15th, making a 10-minute drive take twice as long.

By 9 p.m., however, traffic on 15th clears considerably. Cars don't slowly roll past Frierson like they do at carpool time—they speed past it. It's easy to find yourself speeding down 15th at night if there's no one in your way. When Mitchell arrived, there would have been plenty of moments with no traffic, interrupted by the occasional speeder. The bus stop was on the northwest corner of the intersection, with some trees and shrubs behind it and no nearby streetlights. For someone looking for an easy target just standing in the dark, it was a perfect choice.

It is impossible to know whether Ben saw his murderer before the first shot was fired. Perhaps Donaldson stayed behind the trees and stopped a few steps short of the corner to find a target. As a musician, Ben often had headphones on, so it's possible he never heard him coming; though even if he did it wouldn't have been that unusual for another person to walk up to the bus stop and stand there. Maybe Ben did see him. Maybe he even acknowledged his killer with a nod before looking back in the direction of the bus.

A security camera on Frierson recorded the shooter walking by, and eight minutes later, it captured the sound of the gunshots that killed Mitchell. There are no witnesses to the murder, but perhaps, with Ben facing north toward the bus and Donaldson coming from his left, his first shot was the one that hit him in the left arm. Multiple nearby witnesses noted that they heard Mitchell yell out in pain after the first shot, so it wasn't instantly fatal.

For some reason, after the first shot, Donaldson paused. The audio recording from the camera on Frierson has a few seconds between the first shot and the rest. Did he need to process what he'd just done? He'd been planning this moment for weeks; did he need to process the reality of what it was like to finally pull the trigger and shoot another human being? Or maybe he shot Mitchell from the bushes behind the bus stop, knocking him onto his back, and walked to get closer before firing again.

Regardless of the reason, the pause was brief, and he fired three more times in quick succession. On his feet or on his back, Mitchell faced Donaldson for these shots—he was hit once in the chest and twice in the stomach.

Thirty seconds after the shots were heard by the security camera, it recorded Donaldson running back down Frierson the way he came. At 9:02 p.m., the AT&T cell phone tower in Seminole Heights stopped providing service to his phone, as it was no longer the closest tower. He pulled into the neighborhood at 8:47 p.m., committed a murder, and was gone again in just fifteen minutes.

Neighbors heard the shots and came out to see Mitchell on the ground near the edge of the street. They ran to his aid, trying to stop the bleeding by using their clothes for makeshift tourniquets as he gasped for air. They called police and encouraged Ben to hang on. The first officers on the scene did CPR, and soon after paramedics rushed him to the hospital. Just thirty minutes later, however, Benjamin Mitchell was dead.

I had no idea that our church would have multiple roles to play as the season of the Seminole Heights serial killer unfolded over the next 51 days. They don't teach you in seminary how to lead a church when there's a serial killer at large, and the Bible certainly doesn't address it. However, when it was time for Seminole Heights United Methodist to step up and do our part, we were ready.

I deserve zero credit for having a plan, or any kind of foresight to put a plan in place, that got us ready. It just so happened that the things we felt led to do at Seminole Heights, in the years before a serial killer terrorized our neighborhood, ended up being the things our neighbors needed us to do to serve them when the time came.

You're not going to hear me say anything like, "God knew there was a serial killer coming, and thus led us to do the things we did . . ." Serial killers are not a part of God's plan. What I do know is that God's call upon His church is to always be ready to sacrifice and serve our neighbors well, whether the times are easy or hard, safe or scary. My hope in sharing this story is that other church and community leaders might have the foresight to consider the benefit of some of these steps in their context, which I only realized in hindsight.

A One-Act Play

I LOVE WHEN SOMETHING is said well. One of my favorite things is great TV or movie dialogue—which requires something to be *written* well first, and then *said* well too. I want to hang out someday with the writers from *The West Wing*, *30 Rock*, *New Girl*, or *The Office*. They say stuff well.

I like it even more when I get to say the things well myself, so I became a creative writing major in college. While there's not a sea of employers out there looking for creative writing majors, it just seemed to occupy too much of my soul to cast aside. Eventually I became a church pastor—I thank God for calling me to do something where I get to say things for a living.

Saying things is both my career and my hobby, meaning that I produce a lot of writing that no one will ever read. I know that sounds like torture for those who aren't fans of the language arts, but if you're a writer—I know you get me.

Before I get too far into the story of being a church pastor in a neighborhood victimized by a serial killer, I offer you a one-act play that I wrote not long after I arrived at Seminole Heights. I put it on my blog, and so I think it was seen by all three of my subscribers, but other than that, I resolved myself long ago that it would be one of those pieces that would not see much light of day.

I was about to write a chapter here to share with you the journey I've gone on regarding evangelism. It's important to share this journey with you, because it became a critical element in my interactions with my new neighbors. I would not have been able to have—to enjoy—my relationships with them had the Holy Spirit not set me free from the responsibility to worry about the eternal destiny of those who have not given their lives to Christ.

I know that's a heavy thing to read, as it's also a heavy thing to write. To some, the idea is liberating—to others, blasphemous. To some, reassuring—to others, false teaching. What the Spirit revealed to me, however, was that though it's a heavy thing to hear, and a heavy thing to write; it is a much heavier thing to carry, and it lightens the load considerably to be able to lay it down.

As I was about to write a whole chapter full of Biblical exegesis complimented by a healthy dose of theology, soteriology, and ecclesiology thrown in; I was suddenly reminded of my one-act play.

With apologies to anyone who was excited about all of those—ologies, I think this will be a better approach. To those who groaned and hoped that you'd survive this chapter without having to go to the trouble to look up those words, you're welcome.

To each of you, the lights have been flicked on and off in the lobby. Please make your way to your seats in the theater, and enjoy this production of *Can I Offer You Some Organized Religion?*

> [Casting Note: *In today's production, the role of "Pastor" will be played by Pastor Matt. We regret any inconvenience this may cause. Unfortunately, there are no refunds or exchanges.*]

> [Scene: *Empty stage. There is a microphone on a stand illuminated by a single spotlight. The lighting makes the scene feel like it's in black and white. Footsteps echo as Pastor Matt steps into the light from stage left, stopping at the microphone, hands folded behind his back. A brief whine of feedback is heard, then fades.*]

> **Pastor Matt:** Confession is good for your soul. It's also bad for your reputation.

> I guess everyone has to weigh which one is more important to them sometimes—their soul or their reputation. Today, I'm erring on the side of my soul, so here it is:

I've been that guy you hate.

You know the one I mean. The one you're afraid of winding up next to on an airplane, on a bus, or in an elevator. The one you hope doesn't marry into your family. The one you hope doesn't come knocking on your door or handing you a pamphlet in the mall. The one you hope doesn't get assigned to the cubicle next to you.

I confess I've been the *evangelism* guy. I have *proselytized*.

[*Fast footsteps can be heard. A man in a suit speed walks into the spotlight, whispers in Pastor Matt's ear, and then walks away as quickly as he arrived.*]

Pastor Matt: Oh, um, scratch that last thing. My attorney says it might be ill-advised to admit that. He's gonna get back to me.

Well, in the spirit of *almost* full-disclosure, I admit I *have* started conversations with strangers with the sole hope of convincing them to embrace something whose popularity probably polls about as high as colonoscopies or cockroaches. Yes—I have tried to get people into . . . [*Pastor Matt faces away from the microphone and puts a fist to his mouth while he takes a deep breath. He then returns to the microphone, hand returning behind his back.*]

. . . organized religion.

[*A voice shouts from the audience, stage left.*]

Voice #1: No!

[*A collective gasp rises from the audience. The camera shakes and quickly pans back. Someone loses control of the spotlight, and it clumsily sweeps across the audience to reveal flashes of faces twisted in horror. A baby cries. Someone screams, and someone else faints. A voice cries out.*]

Voice #2: Is there a doctor in the house?

[*Finally, a stampede of footsteps erupts as people rush for the doors. As the last footsteps die away, the camera and spotlight return to their original positions, and Pastor Matt puts a hand up above his eyes in an attempt to block the bright stage light and see if anyone is still left in the audience. He can't tell, so he shrugs, and continues on as if there were.*]

Pastor Matt: So I guess I don't have to tell you that there aren't many people in the market for organized religion.

[*Fast footsteps are heard again, and the attorney walks behind Pastor Matt holding a briefcase and wearing an overcoat. He stops, looks at Pastor Matt with disgust, puts on a hat, and continues on out of the spotlight. The footsteps get farther away, until the sound of a door closing can be heard from stage right. Pastor Matt turns back to the microphone.*]

Pastor Matt: See what I mean?

I tried to make it fun. I tried to tell everybody how nice heaven is, and how bad hell is, and how all you had to do to punch your ticket for heaven was to pray a prayer and tell God that you were accepting Jesus Christ as your savior. Then you come to church and hang out with others who had prayed the same prayer, and you learn more about Jesus and you do fun things together and sometimes you do mission trips where you do nice things for people so that they'll listen to us tell them about how they can go to heaven too.

Organized religion can be fun. There are good speakers that tell stories and jokes and help inspire us to tell more people about Jesus. We have bands and choirs and church organs and other kinds of music. Sometimes there's skits and dancers. And we go on ski trips and have youth lock-ins and other fun stuff too.

Sure, there are times when it's not fun, and you'd rather do something else, but that's when it helps to remember that everybody who isn't a part of our organized religion is probably going to hell, so if you care about them, you'll keep on going and keep on telling people about it.

It worked sometimes. It worked often enough, actually, that I started to think I was pretty good at it. So I went to school—seminary—so that I could get a job as an actual organizer of religion.

While I was there, though, I started noticing something. When people stop going to churches where the organized religion happens, it's harder to get people to give money to keep them going. You can't hire as many people as you used to. You can't buy as many Christian books, or as much Christian music as you used to. You can't hire as many church building companies, or buy as much church furniture as you used to. You also can't find as many places to work as an organizer of religion as you used to. Organized religion starts going out of business.

So we started talking about how to keep churches from closing, and how to get more people to come so more churches could stay open so we could keep the buildings Christians like and the staff members employed to run programs that Christians like. And even though we kept saying that we were doing all of this because we care about people's souls, it seemed more and more like we talked about how we missed the way the churches used to be when there were more people in them, and how expensive it is to repair and operate the big fancy buildings we built back when there were more people there giving more money. I started to not like organized religion while I was actually learning to organize it.

Fortunately, while I was in seminary I also learned about Jesus. I was struck by how little time he spent keeping people who were already in organized religion entertained. I was struck by how little time he spent thinking about how to keep things the way they were. I was struck by his imagination, and how he talked about what we could create here on Earth if we became people who loved God and loved our neighbor. I was struck by how rarely he seemed to be concerned with getting people to heaven when they die, and how often he seemed concerned with getting people to experience heaven right here while we're still alive. In fact, when Heaven comes up in the Bible, it's rarely a *destination* for the people and things of God—it's where the people and things of God *come from* to make this world more like Heaven.

Jesus' imagination began to make me imagine too. What would be possible if I organized religion so that it cared about the things Jesus cared about? How much time would we spend thinking about how to put on a good enough show to draw a crowd of paying customers so we could keep the place open? How much time would we spend thinking about how to get people into heaven when they die? Hardly any.

What would be possible if we organized religion to create heaven right here in our neighborhood? What would it be like to live in a place of love, kindness, grace, charity, encouragement, service, and hope? As I finished seminary I found myself gaining new hope and new excitement for the purpose and possibilities for organized religion, for the church—but first, a confession is in order. To all of you who hate organized religion and want nothing to do with the church, here it is:

[*Pastor Matt again puts his hand above his eyes to see if there's anyone in the audience, but he still can't tell. He sighs as his arms fall to his sides, assuming that the room is probably empty.*]

Pastor Matt: You don't need the church. The church needs you.

It's supposed to create heaven on earth, and it can't do it without you.

It can only do it if it *is* you.

[*He puts his hand up one more time to look around, then looks up at the ceiling, closes his eyes, and smiles. He takes a deep cleansing breath, and speaks quietly to himself, though the microphone catches it.*]

Pastor Matt: Whaddya know? It *is* good for the soul.

[*Pastor Matt puts his hands in his pockets, looks around once more, smiles, and walks off, stage left. Footsteps fade until silent. After a few seconds of silence, a seat in the audience creaks from someone standing up. Footsteps walk to the back door, which opens. A streetlight outside causes the silhouette of someone in the doorway to project on the back curtain of the stage. They stop, turn, and look back toward the stage, and then exit. The light from outside shrinks as the door swings toward closing. The light disappears, and the sound of the door closing echoes through the empty room for a moment, and then falls silent. End scene.*]

I've been asked by a couple of the (very few) people who read this one-act play on my blog: Who was the person who leaves at the end—the one who'd stayed behind to hear the rest of the play when everyone else left?

If you were to ask a Sunday school class, someone would probably guess "Jesus!" While you're never supposed to say that Jesus is the wrong answer, well, that's the wrong answer.

The person isn't a specific individual—they're a reminder that sharing the Good News about Jesus is never wasted. You may think that no one is listening, but you'd be surprised how often someone later on will tell you that what you said made them think, and how it made them want to hear more.

Starting in School

MY FIRST CLERGY APPOINTMENT was serving as the associate pastor at Hyde Park United Methodist near Downtown Tampa in 2007. I didn't realize it at the time, but we started "becoming Seminole Heights" long before we lived there.

My wife, Susan is a school social worker. Good school social workers accomplish more of the work of the Kingdom of God in one day than some churches do in a year. They quickly become a critical safety net for students, teachers, staff, and administrators in any school to which they're assigned. While I was only in my second year at Hyde Park, Susan became the school social worker at Seminole Heights Elementary, located across the street from Seminole Heights United Methodist, years before I would serve there as the pastor.

The degree to which I have married over my head is hard to overstate. Susan graduated summa cum laude with her bachelor of social work degree (BSW), and she got straight As in graduate school, getting her masters degree in social work (MSW) on top of that. She has won every "Employee of the [insert time period here]" award there is at every job she's ever had. I frequently tell her that she's so gifted and such a hard worker that she could be doing something way more lucrative so that I could stay home and be her house husband. The problem is that there just isn't much money to be made in the helping-kids-who-are-in-terrible-situations industry, but that's her calling. So, no house husband for her.

Little did we know, however, that Susan's commitment to professionalism and her heart for hurting kids laid the groundwork for our season of ministry in Seminole Heights. As you can imagine, she became indispensable to the principal at Seminole Heights Elementary, Dr. Jackie Masters. Susan seemed to be on everybody's speed dial when trouble arose at home for a student that prevented them from being able to learn.

In addition to Susan's season of establishing a good reputation for the Horan name with our future neighbors, our daughters, Jenna and Ashley were both on the City of Tampa Gymnastics Team, which happened to practice almost every day at the Wayne Papy Athletic Center, in Seminole Heights. So for about four years before we ever lived there, Susan or I drove through the neighborhood just about every day to drive them back and forth to practice.

> We befriended the principals in our public school zone.

I became a middle school English teacher after college. I later went to graduate school to get a master's degree in educational administration, which is the degree you get if you want to become a school principal someday. Not long after graduating, however, I felt God calling me to take a job in youth ministry, and then to pursue ordained ministry. At first I thought it would have been nice for God to have told me that before I went to graduate school for something else, but we've talked it over since then and we're good now.

What this degree did was to give me a burden to care for the education professionals in my neighborhood. During my first week at Seminole Heights, I paid visits to the principals at Hillsborough High School, Memorial Middle School, and Seminole Heights Elementary School, which resulted in some of the most important relationships I had during my season of ministry there.

You've Got to Be Kidding Me

On my first official day in the office, Tuesday, July 2, 2013, someone who worked for the *Tampa Bay Times* called. She said she used to attend the church and had a friend who still attended, and was excited about their new pastor. She wanted to send a reporter to the church to interview me and write a story in the paper about the church, so I jumped at the chance for the free publicity. The reporter came by, and we chatted for about 20 minutes. As she was leaving, she said that she wanted to get a photo of me in front of the church in case there was room for a picture to go along with the article. So I stood on the front steps and smiled, just in case.

On the way into the office later that week, I passed an office volunteer who asked me, "Did you see your big article?"

I'd almost forgotten about it until she asked, but I did notice the word "big" in there. I hadn't been around long enough to know who the sarcastic people were yet, and I wasn't sure about her. I assumed sarcasm though, since Tampa is a big place, and articles about pastors' new jobs at churches probably wouldn't rise to the "big article" level.

"No I didn't. How did we sound?"

"See for yourself," she replied, handing me the local section, folded in half. I took it, unfolded it, and my jaw dropped.

"You should get a frame for that," she said like a proud parent. "That's a great picture."

There I was, staring back at myself from the front page of the local section of the paper. The main headline read, "New Pastor Takes the Helm at Local Church." I remembered the reporter saying she wanted to get a picture "in case there was room," but now I wasn't sure there was room for the article because of the huge picture of me. It was so big you had to hold up the whole front page because it continued beneath the fold.

I think my stunned silence eventually got awkward. She asked, "What do you think?"

I managed to unparalyze my face and said, "You've got to be kidding me. I haven't even done anything yet!"

Needless to say, I heard from a few different people that day. The article was emailed to me from several people who read it online. I had copies of it brought to me in the office by church members in case I hadn't seen it, and many more brought with them to church on Sunday. On the other hand, my clergy colleagues couldn't think of bishops even getting an article in the paper like that, and they enjoyed telling me how honored they felt to know someone so famous.

After my friends stopped calling, emailing, and texting; I started getting phone calls and emails that I didn't see coming. Apparently there are a lot of companies in the business of scanning newspapers for flattering articles, contacting the flattered person, and offering to display the article for you in a variety of different ways for exorbitant amounts of money. I suppose the people that usually get flattering articles written about them in the paper can afford to have them treated and preserved, mounted and framed, decoupaged onto a piece of decorative wood, turned into t-shirts, made into magnets for the side of your car, blown up into poster-sized wall art, or even printed on an edible sheet to put on the top of a cake.

While I passed on these offers, I knew we needed to leverage the attention. I was pretty embarrassed by me and my little church making such a huge splash in the paper when I knew pastors of far bigger churches in the area who could have easily filled that picture and that article with news of their many accomplishments. However, it was Seminole Heights United Methodist who had a reporter in the right place at the right time on a slow enough news day to make us headline news, so once it happened, we could have either waited for the attention to pass and gone back to normal, or made the most of it.

Though I wanted to collect every copy from every newsstand, hide them in a basement, and ignore it with all of its accompanying lofty expectations, we posted it on the church's *Facebook* page and *Twitter* account, and then watched as members began to proudly click "Share," happy to see good news about their church in the paper again after

> People really want to be proud of their church, and have some reasons to brag about it.

many years of anxiety about their decline. The Sunday before I got there, we had about 60 people in attendance. By the Sunday morning after the article, those 60 were back, looking around with glee at the additional 40 or so now sitting around them.

Hyde Park had given me a couple weeks off in between my two appointments, so by the time I got to my first Sunday at Seminole Heights, I hadn't preached in almost a month. I was pent up and ready to go with a sermon I'd been writing ever since I learned I was going there three months before, and it was good. The moment came, I gave it everything I had, and I think that would have been one of the best sermons of my life if it wasn't for one problem. The air conditioning in the sanctuary stopped working on that hot Florida day in early July, and some quick-thinking ushers retrieved two large industrial metal fans from storage in the basement. They really helped cool the place off, but also sounded like jet engines, so nobody heard a word I said.

Fortunately, those in attendance had extra help fighting off the heat that morning. Many of them brought the local section of Friday's paper with them to church, and as I looked out on the congregation during my sermon, I noticed that they seemed to make great hand-held fans, which was one more unexpected benefit from the great press we'd gotten that first week.

See that? I was helping already.

Just Ask

AT SOME POINT IN my upbringing, I was taught that it's not enough to open a fortune cookie and just read the fortune. I learned that to really get the most out of the experience, you had to add, "... with a barrel of monkeys." You have to admit that learning "You will soon make a new friend" doesn't sound nearly as much fun as "You will soon make a new friend *with a barrel of monkeys.*"

Of course, at some point I learned that you can really add any prepositional phrase to the end of the sage words from your fortune cookie to increase their pizazz. Perhaps "You will soon make a new friend *near some elephants,*" or "You will soon make a new friend *on the London Bridge,*" or "You will soon make a new friend *on the International Space Station.*" Depending on the phrase you add, that fortune could become even more fortunate.

I discovered early on after becoming a follower of Jesus that Christians often do the same thing when it comes to loving our neighbors. We'll do an easter egg hunt for the neighborhood, but while giving the instructions to eager kids white-knuckling their baskets, we're also going to tell you about Jesus for a few minutes. We'll do a neighborhood Christmas event, but there's an offering basket on the way out just in case you're feeling generous. We'll sell you a pumpkin from our pumpkin patch, and here's a schedule of our worship service times.

Moving from Hyde Park United Methodist with over a thousand people in worship every Sunday to Seminole Heights, which had about sixty every Sunday, obviously took some getting used to. No one ever talked about Hyde Park closing down—there were about 20–30 new guests every week, and a dozen or more people joined every couple months. The challenge was finding places to fit them into small groups and serving opportunities.

At Seminole Heights, however, people had already been talking about closing for years when I got there. In the minds of the congregation, the need for new people was about one thing, and everyone seemed to phrase it the same: "keeping the doors open."

I'd seen a movie called *The Invention of Lying* before our move, which asked viewers to step into a world in which it lying didn't exist—that is, until the main character invents it.

So, for fun I toyed with the idea of a completely honest church invitation.

"Hello, we're going to have to close our church if more people don't start attending, so would you please do us a solid and come on by this Sunday?"

"Hi! We feel a lot better about ourselves when our church is crowded, so would you mind doing us a favor and giving us a try this weekend at 9 or 11 a.m.?"

"Hi, we need more people to come to our church and give more money so we won't have to lay anybody off. Would you please join us this Sunday?"

"We believe everybody needs Jesus, but it makes us uncomfortable telling people that in person, so we hope that this invitation stuck in your windshield wiper will do the trick."

Part of me really wanted to try that marketing campaign purely for the entertainment value, but I didn't have the courage to go for it.

Still, I'd become tired of the bait and switch—fooling people into coming to hear about Jesus by promising them something else. Maybe it's because of all the people I know who have pretty good reasons to want nothing to do with the church. I didn't want to lie to anyone, and I didn't want to trick anyone. I wanted to treat them like they're as smart as they are and level with them. I wanted to be honest.

I admit that we got to this in the wrong order. As a church of Jesus Christ, there should have been abundant clarity about why we were there and the difference we were called to make; but "keeping the doors open" had become such a pervasive worry that there just wasn't a whole lot else on the heart, minds, and souls at Seminole Heights.

Since I was going to require that we be honest, we would have to tell people to come to the church because we needed them, but we couldn't expect anyone to show up to keep us open.

The difference that Seminole Heights United Methodist made in our neighborhood would have to be one that mattered to the neighborhood. So, my first step was to forbid anyone from talking anymore about "keeping the doors open," "surviving," "stayin' alive," or any other similar phrase. We were not going to exist for the sake of existing, we were going to exist to have an impact on our neighborhood.

> We eliminated "staying open" as a goal for the church.

For my first few weeks the congregation heard me say, "If there's a church of Jesus Christ in your neighborhood, it should make your life noticeably better whether you're a part of it or not." We then had a series of meetings open to the whole congregation to get into groups and accomplish our second step –brainstorming the biggest problems facing the neighborhood.

Now if we were going to ask for our neighbors to help us with solving these problems, they needed to believe that they actually were problems. So, I began walking around the neighborhood, knocking on doors, introducing myself, and asking them one question: "How could Seminole Heights United Methodist be a good neighbor to you?" I asked residents, business owners, local school administrators, and everybody I could find.

Oddly enough, people struggled with the question. I discovered that not only is the church really good at baiting and switching—doing nice things for the neighborhood only to get them to attend, volunteer, give, or change their behavior in return—we've also trained people outside of the church to expect it. People I spoke to would start giving me ideas, and then they'd veer into how their ideas might end up leading people to get involved with the church. They expected it so much that, when I didn't say it, they started saying it for me. They struggled to understand how being a good neighbor could be a goal for a church, rather than a strategy to accomplish something else.

In response, I said, "Well, anyone is welcome to join us for anything we do, whether on a Sunday or any other day, but we're not looking to be good neighbors to get more members. We're looking for ways to be good neighbors because that's what we're supposed to be." Most of those I visited were Biblically aware enough to recall that there was something in there about loving your neighbor. They'd just never been approached by a person of faith without being pushed to attend something, give something, do something, or stop doing something. In fact, they found the approach so refreshing that most people I met told me that they'd like to come and visit. And many of them did.

> We asked our neighbors what they needed, and they told us.

As more and more of our projects and ministries came from the suggestions of our neighbors, we found more of our neighbors interested in helping them become successful by getting involved, spreading the word, volunteering, and contributing financially. The neighborhood knows what the neighborhood needs. If you ask them, they'll give you some great ideas, and since it was their idea, they just might feel some responsibility to help it succeed.

The Atheist and the Christmas Trees

ONE OF THE BEST responses to my good neighbor question was from a young guy of about 25 who lived two blocks north of the church. I knocked, and he opened his door.

"Hey, what's going on?"

"Hi, my name is Matt, and I just became the pastor at Seminole Heights United Methodist down the street."

"Oh, hold on, bro," he interrupted, "I appreciate you stopping by, but I'm an atheist."

Now, I admit that my next line wasn't my best. I adjusted before the next house, but this time I said, "Oh, I'm not here to invite you to the church—well, I mean, not that I wouldn't be glad for you to come and give it a try sometime if you like. Sorry, that's pretty terrible coming from a church pastor. What I meant to say is that I've been walking around asking people about what the church could be doing to become a good neighbor to those who live around it. So, I'm just here asking for advice."

"Oh," he said. I'm not sure which he found more surprising, the question or the non-invitation, but he actually gave me one of the most important suggestions I received. "Well, honestly, I wouldn't mind having a place around here to buy a Christmas tree without having to go to a big chain hardware store."

I wish I'd gotten his name to thank him, because I wrote that idea down, and a few months later the first annual Seminole

Heights Christmas Tree Lighting and Christmas Tree Lot opened for business.

We listened to our neighbors, and committed to be in prayer, listening for the Spirit to lead us. What we discerned over those first few months at Seminole Heights was that the main needs of the neighborhood were community gathering events and support for the local schools, especially Seminole Heights Elementary and Memorial Middle School.

Next, we had to figure out what we had to offer that could be useful in these two areas. While we didn't have a lot of people or money, we did have something awesome—the corner of Central and Hanna.

The church is located on a fantastic corner in the neighborhood. We had an amazing crossing guard—Mr. Randy—who high fived every kid that walked by on the way to school, and was one of the coolest people I've ever met.

The school was on the northeast corner, a row of great shops that included a delicious bakery and a popular pet supply store was on the southwest, a little shop that made candles and t-shirts on another on the northwest, and we were on the southeast. Whenever one of our neighbors on the corner had an event, we insisted on being the official parking lot.

> We found the intersection of what our neighborhood needed and what we had to offer.

We thought that was a great way to be a good neighbor, though I admit we did occasionally put invitations to our events on the windshield wipers. After all, good neighbors invite each other over every once in a while, right?

Seminole Heights United Methodist was the official overflow parking lot for all Seminole Heights Elementary events, as well as the morning drop-off lot for moms and dads who were walking their kids to school. Whenever they would ask if it was okay for cars to park there, we reminded them that they were doing us a favor by letting us be good neighbors, as that's how our church could become more like Jesus.

Every year Seminole Heights Elementary had an event called the Walk to Hillsborough. It was a day when the students would all make the mile or so walk south to Hillsborough High School to give them the long view of their school career, knowing that there were bigger and bigger things in store for them as they moved along. Every year on the morning of the walk, we would set up our portable speakers on the church's front porch and play music to pump up the kids as they walked by us on the way south, and again on their way back. It was the easiest thing in the world to do, and the kids danced on by us and loved it every time.

Our huge property was the best thing we had going, and we made the most of that too. We had movies on the lawn, set up a temporary fence and had "dog park days," and hosted food truck rallies with live music from our worship band. We had a big arts and crafts sale, and hosted an annual event during which animal rescue organizations came together for an informational fair where everyone in the neighborhood brought their dog and had a great time. We even loaned people folding tables and chairs to use at their homes for when company came at Thanksgiving. Everything we owned became an opportunity to be a good neighbor.

The biggest splashes on our campus were a huge pumpkin patch, a "Trunk or Treat" for Halloween, and the Christmas tree lot, kicked off by the Seminole Heights Christmas Tree Lighting on the first Sunday night of Advent. The whole neighborhood would bring lawn chairs and blankets, sit around the tree, and sing Christmas carols led by our choir and worship band. We'd then have all of the kids come and do a countdown, and light up the tree to cheers from the whole crowd. It drew hundreds of people, and got bigger each year.

We were the official venue of all of the elementary school's music performances, which just about filled the sanctuary each time. The music programs by our preschoolers were also a big hit, partly because of how many times I told the congregation that, if they love Jesus, they'll be there to cheer on the preschoolers. I was glad to see that a lot of our members loved Jesus.

The most monstrous crowd we ever drew was during a fundraiser for a local radio station. They managed to book Amy Goodman of *Democracy Now!* She's a radio and podcast host, and directs their independent news reporting organization. She is a highly sought-after speaker.

This isn't really a book for fire marshals, but if you happen to be one, I apologize for the Amy Goodman fundraiser. We had standing room only *in the balcony*. We added seats everywhere we could shoehorn one more in, and even more people were listening on the radio station and on *Facebook Live*. When I stepped up to the pulpit to welcome everyone, point out where the bathrooms are, etc., I just stood there for a moment looking at everybody, took out my phone, and then said, "Hi, I'm Matt, the pastor here at Seminole Heights United Methodist, and, before we begin, would you mind if I take a picture of you all filling up the sanctuary like this to send it to my parents and show them what a big success I am? Just make your best, I'm-at-church-listening-to-Matt's-riveting-sermon face for me for sec . . . excellent. Thank you so much."

I still have that picture on my phone.

After a couple of years of this approach, you could ask anyone around, whether they attended on Sundays or not, about the reputation of Seminole Heights United Methodist, and they'd tell you something like, "That church really cares about our neighborhood." People at our various events or at events we hosted for organizations in our sanctuary would often say things like, "You know, Pastor Matt, I'm not really into church, but if I was, I would definitely come to your church."

I would then offer, "Well, if you ever need one, I would be glad to be your pastor." I got to a point where I said that pretty reflexively, without thinking about whether they'd take me up on it, but a lot of them did.

A question often came up when people would use our space or equipment: How much do you charge?

When I was at Hyde Park, I did premarital counseling for a young woman named Candice and her husband, Matt. After their wedding they moved to Seminole Heights, and on my first Sunday there, I was as pleasantly surprised to see them in attendance as they were to see that I was their new pastor.

I allowed Candice to repay me for my high-quality counseling by serving as the chairperson of the church's Finance Committee for what probably felt like several years because of my answer to questions like that.

> We didn't charge people or groups to use our space.

In hindsight, we probably would have brought in a little more income had we created a set fee schedule for the use of our spaces or equipment, so I'm not entirely sure my way was the right way. However, there was something powerful in being able to say to someone, "There's no charge. Having neighbors over is what good neighbors do. Make yourself at home." I think there was something powerful in hearing it too—it probably sounded a lot like grace.

That said, I'm pretty sure Candice and I are even now.

The Eagles

As a product of Philadelphia, PA, I am a die-hard Eagles fan. When I called to make an appointment to meet with the principal, Dr. Masters, her recorded voice greeted me when the phone system picked up, thanking me for calling Seminole Heights Elementary, "the Home of the Eagles."

Did God inspire someone long ago to choose the Eagles as the mascot at Seminole Heights Elementary to add one more layer of reassurance that I was sent to the right place? I kind of doubt it, but do I remember looking up when I heard that and telling Him, "Okay, now you're just showing off."

As I'd hoped, Susan Horan was still revered as the gold standard of social workers in the eyes of the principal and many of the staff at the school, even though she'd been reassigned to someplace new a couple years prior. They welcomed me from day one, and invited me to be a part of many different facets of their work. I was invited to facilitate the "All Pro Dads" program in the mornings during breakfast, to join their school advisory council, and was even invited to help conduct interviews as they sought a new assistant principal!

One of my favorite experiences at Seminole Heights came through this partnership. After the students and teachers finished their statewide standardized testing and all of that pressure was behind them, I invited them over to our sanctuary for a sing-along concert. We put the words to popular songs the kids knew on the screens, and blasted them from the sound system. I didn't know what to expect, but whether it was "Let it Go" from *Frozen*, or songs by Justin Timberlake, Katy Perry, or Taylor Swift; the kids danced in their seats and sang each song at the top of their lungs. The teachers were stationed around the room to enforce "church behavior," but before long many of them were singing right along, having fun with the kids that they'd grown to love after spending the last few months pushing, pulling, and dragging them toward standardized testing success.

The next year we added some short, funny video segments in between the songs, and my last year as pastor I challenged the three male teachers on the staff to a lip sync battle to Vanilla Ice's *Ice Ice Baby*, as I assumed they'd all know the words. They didn't disappoint.

There were two brief conversations I had with teachers as the students filed out of the sing-long concert I'll never forget.

The first said, "I didn't know you were allowed to play Taylor Swift in church."

I replied with a wink, "As long as the pastor is okay with it."

"And your pastor is okay with it?"

She clearly didn't know I was the pastor, so I just went with it. "So far!"

"Well, he must be an unusual pastor."

I suppressed some laughter at that. "Yeah, he gets that a lot."

The next teacher in line overheard that exchange, and when the previous one had moved out of earshot, she asked, "Aren't you the pastor?"

I smiled and nodded. "Yeah, I am."

She laughed. "Okay, that's hilarious."

The second was a minute or two later. She said, "I've always believed that you should only play church music in church, but when the songs started and you played Taylor Swift, I thought maybe you were doing this to get kids back in church. Is that why you're doing this?"

I said, "Nope. Just trying to be good, fun neighbors."

She didn't seem to approve of that. "Hmm . . . well that's very interesting."

The next teacher after her shook her head. "That was a great answer," she said. "Don't worry about her—just shake it off."

That was a nicely done Taylor Swift pun, in case you missed it. I'd bet she was a good teacher.

The pastor's office window looks out at Seminole Heights Elementary. I heard every loudspeaker announcement, every fire drill, and every dismissal bell. Over my years there the life of the church and the life of the school came to feel like one in the same. They made me feel like I was a part of the staff of the school, and I'm humbled by their acceptance to this day.

One thing that became automatic was that, if we ever saw emergency vehicles pull up to the school, I would call to check and see if it would help for me to come over. They always appreciated it, and even missed it if we didn't notice for some reason and didn't call! It happened only a few times in the five years I served there, and all but one of those times they thanked me, but said it wasn't necessary.

There was that one time, though, when the receptionist said, "Yeah, Pastor Matt, you'd better come over."

At some point in Keith's development, before he was even born, a blood vessel formed in his brain with an abnormality. It would become an aneurysm—a bulge that could burst at any moment in his life, or perhaps never. It happened to burst while he was sitting in his first grade class at Seminole Heights Elementary School, just after lunch time on a Thursday afternoon.

He told his teacher, Erin, that he had a headache. She asked him if he'd like to go down to the nurse, or if he'd like to lie down on the cushions in the class' reading area, and he opted for the cushions. A few minutes later, he began vomiting, and then lost consciousness. Erin called for help and then stayed with him, having the presence of mind to get her class out of the room and into a neighboring first grade teacher's room to minimize their exposure to their classmate in distress.

I walked in as the ambulance was leaving. The receptionist took me to a room where Erin was seated with the school psychologist and a couple others who had been with Keith before he was taken to the hospital. I knew that the sooner she could organize the adrenaline-scattered thoughts in her head, the better for her own healing. I told her how sorry I was, and asked her if she could tell me what happened. I listened as she and a couple others who had been there shared and processed the experience, all the while wondering how he was doing. They struggled with being in the middle of it one second, and then having no idea what was happening the next.

When Erin's fiancé arrived, I broke away and called the chaplain's office at St. Joseph's Hospital where Keith had been taken. The chaplain on call was great, and he and I managed to make a plan with Keith's mom to have Erin come and visit him in the hospital. Keith loved his teacher and told his mom about her all the time, so she was glad to have her come over. The chaplain later told me the decision had been made that Keith would not be able to recover from the burst aneurysm, but he was still on life support so that his organs could be donated to others in need. Keith's heart is currently still beating in a little girl's body today, one of 14 different patients who received organ or tissue donations from him.

I went back into the room where Erin and her fiancé were, and explained the situation—how there there was nothing else they could do to help him recover, that he'd be on life support, and what the scene in the room would look like. I wasn't sure she'd want to see him like that, but she didn't hesitate, and said she wanted to go. I went ahead of them to visit Keith's mom and dad, and then met Erin and a couple other staff from the school in the lobby to walk them up.

Erin first hugged Keith's mom, and then went over to the bed of the little boy who had walked into her classroom that morning like any other day. For some reason, my most distinct memory of that moment was when she stepped up next to the bed, looked down at him, and compassionately said, "Hey, buddy." I contrasted that for a moment with the way the nuns at my elementary school called me "Mr. Horan." I'm pretty sure Erin's way was better.

That was the first moment my day had stopped since seeing those emergency vehicles pull up to the school, and I had a few minutes to reflect on what had happened. It hit me that I didn't know anyone in that hospital room very well five hours ago, but here I was, invited into such an intensely personal, painful thing. Parents losing a child. A teacher losing a student.

Once again I was humbled by the privilege that this school staff team bestowed upon me, inviting the church pastor from next door to be one of them, to be a part of their team as they did the vital work they do on the easiest of days, let alone the unbearable work they do on days like that one.

We gathered to pray around Keith before Erin and the others from the school went home. Sometimes when I'm praying out loud, I become keenly aware of the people who are hearing the prayer, and I need to pause to take a quiet moment to focus my words at God, rather than at those listening around me. I'd prayed prayers during which I failed to do that before—where I was really talking to the people around me rather than to God. I trust that God still received those words, but they always felt flat to me after the fact.

Far more good comes from me taking these people with me to stand before God and let them hear me talking to Him, so they know He can handle our grief, our questions, our anger, and our honest disappointment when it feels like his omnipotence has failed us. If they hear me express it to Him, perhaps they'll learn it's okay to express it to Him as well. Therefore, I need that quiet moment. Sometimes, it's a longer moment than others—even awkwardly so. I don't remember what I said that day, but I remember that pause before a prayer was one of my longest.

Once they left, I went to say goodbye to Keith's mom and dad, and they asked if I would be willing to officiate Keith's funeral, and hold it at Seminole Heights United Methodist. His mom said, "It feels right—you're like the school's pastor, after all." I think I felt more humbled and honored by that than just about anything anybody has said to me in my ministry career.

I can't say I saw this coming. I can't say that the efforts to get to know and help and serve them—to be their neighbor—were done in order to be ready for this. Truly, no one is ever ready for the death of a child. We were ready to be there for the school, however, because before that, we'd decided that above all, we were going to be good neighbors.

Our daughter, Ashley, was a fourth grader at Seminole Heights Elementary that year, so we got the phone call from Dr. Masters that went out to the whole student body. Throughout the day on Friday, Keith had been giving new life and new hope to families across the Tampa Bay area by literally giving himself to 14 other people. When that work was finished, he breathed his last, and over 400 phones rang across the neighborhood with the sad news.

"Dear Seminole Heights Students and Parents, Tonight I have to make a call to you that no principal ever wants to make, because earlier this evening, our family lost an Eagle . . ."

The Murder of Monica Hoffa

MONICA HOFFA FINISHED HER shift at the International House of Pancakes and headed home to her house in Seminole Heights on Wednesday night, October 11th. She took an Uber home with a co-worker, who was dropped off first. She then came home, dropped off some items she'd purchased at a Family Dollar earlier in the day, and made plans to meet her friend Corey, who was driving in from St. Petersburg. She was going to walk a couple blocks west and meet him as he drove up Nebraska Avenue.

The first sign of trouble came at 8:39 p.m., when Corey called to tell her that he was three minutes away. He noticed that she seemed distracted and in a hurry, and finally told him, "Okay, I gotta go," and hung up. He wondered what the hurry was, and why she had to hang up. He figured he'd be able to ask her soon.

Police still don't have an exact timeline of the murder. The prevailing theory held by neighbors and journalists is that she noticed Donaldson following her at some point before the phone call. He has an odd walk, and it would have been amplified if he was walking quickly to try to catch up to her. It would have been pretty obvious to her that he was on a mission, and not just a guy out for a stroll. When Corey called, she was already trying to outpace Donaldson, with Nebraska Avenue visible just three blocks ahead, so her seemingly hurried and distracted tone made sense.

It seems like she realized, while on the phone with Corey, that she wasn't going to get to Nebraska Avenue before he caught up to her, and decided to make a run for it. Donaldson gave chase, and as they neared the intersection of New Orleans and 11th Street, he figured he was close enough, and took two shots at her. Both missed—one hit a car parked in a driveway nearby, and the other went through the wall of a garage.

The sound of the gunshots sent Monica running off of the road and into an overgrown drainage pond full of tall weeds and grass. He followed her and fired again, fatally hitting her twice in the back and once in the neck.

Again, there's no official timeline endorsed by investigators. What's clear is that Corey called at 8:39 p.m., Donaldson's cell phone left the area at 8:42 p.m., and by 8:45 p.m., officers were responding to reports of gunfire near the intersection. Without really knowing what they were looking for, they didn't find anything. They didn't find Monica, who was lying on her back on an unlit corner concealed by thick, overgrown weeds; nor did they find her murderer, who had vanished once again.

Two days later, on the morning of October 13th, a city work crew arrived as scheduled to mow the dried up, overgrown drainage pond on the corner of East New Orleans and 11th Avenue. Not long after, they called police and summoned them to the same intersection they'd searched a couple nights before. This time, in broad daylight, they saw what couldn't be seen before—that just a few days later, and just a couple blocks away, there had been another murder in Seminole Heights.

Police Chief Brian Dugan stood before news reporters later on to share that, while there was no evidence that the two victims knew each other, Benjamin Mitchell and Monica Hoffa had both been killed with the same gun. In addition, he showed video footage from a security camera on Frierson St. from the night of Mitchell's murder. The video camera captured someone walking toward the murder, and then running away from it minutes later. He very much wanted to meet them.

That Yellow Church

WITHOUT HESITATION I CAN say that the large, yellow brick home of Seminole Heights United Methodist Church is one of my favorite places on the planet. Even though its air conditioning failed me on my first Sunday (and a few more times after that), even though the complexities of its nearly 100-year-old plumbing summoned me on multiple occasions to mop up human waste, even though it was a magnet for wasp nests in the summer, and even though the slope in the sanctuary was so steep that people sat in the back more out of a fear of falling than simply because that's the United Methodist tradition; I loved being there.

I loved how old it was. I loved how many people had been there before. I loved how it had been a part of the neighborhood as long as the neighborhood had been there. I loved the old pictures of it, like the one with a 1954 Buick Skylark parked alongside on Hanna Avenue, back when it was a cobblestone road. I loved how there were so many people who could tell me where buildings and trees and houses used to be. I loved how the congregation found ways to fix things themselves, and how if they had to call someone to come and fix something, there was a little feeling of defeat. I loved how they were all so well versed in the little nuances in getting things to work, like which switches to turn on in the right order to recycle the air conditioning and get it to come back on when it was trying to take the summer off.

I loved perusing the library cabinets full of Sunday school attendance books, and finding the names of current 90-year-old members listed in a roster from the young couples class in the 1950's who still attended Seminole Heights every Sunday.

I loved the folding movie theater seats that were donated to the church when it was being constructed that still have racks underneath for wide-brimmed hats to be stored during the movie. I loved the way the wood stain on the corners of the pulpit was worn down by the pastors who had gripped it for almost 100 years before me. I loved hearing them tell me about the memorable moments that happened in this room and that room, or how it used to be decorated, or how they used to have a pool table and shuffleboard court in the fellowship ("Allen") hall, named for their founding pastor who'd written a book about ministry that was long on charming stories and surprisingly short on political correctness.

> I came to love the church's story.

The place was a time capsule. You could find church bulletins from the 1950s. There were pictures of Jesus or John Wesley hanging in the same spot they were originally placed that were donated by founding families of the church. If a wall had a big enough dent in it from a furniture-moving mishap or a youth group game gone awry, there's no telling what layers of paint or wallpaper might be revealed. Plaques on the wall from when the church was founded as Seminole Heights Methodist Episcopal Church, South are still visible at the church entrance. I found commemorative plates and church directories from the 1970s, which contained photos of young parents who were now grandparents.

There was one architectural oddity I could never quite figure out. There is a small arch on the roof, maybe six feet wide and ten feet tall, placed in a way that a chimney might be placed on a building with a fireplace. I wondered if it had perhaps been a chimney at one point, but there had never been a fireplace in the church as far as I could tell. The oldest pictures of the sanctuary had the arch in them, so it seems like it has always been there. The funny thing is that, while no one recalls a church bell ever hanging from it, everyone has always called it "the bell tower."

I wondered if, perhaps, at some point during the initial construction, there was an intention to include a bell tower with a working bell. Maybe the founders called it that, and while the bell never came to be, the name of the arch stuck with subsequent generations. Upon further inspection (I loved solving architectural mysteries in that place), I discovered an odd open space on the third floor underneath the bell tower that seemed without purpose. Was that intended to be the loft, where someone would have climbed up and pulled the ropes to sound the bells? No one knows for sure, but it didn't take me long to become convinced that Seminole Heights United Methodist was meant to have church bells, and it wouldn't be complete without them.

Fittingly, our staff-parish relations team and board of trustees had been discussing ways to commemorate the kind of anniversary the likes of which may never be seen again. Our music director, Judy Colvin, was nearing her 40th year on staff. To me, that kind of career belongs in the Hall of Fame next to Cal Ripken, Jr's record of 2,632 consecutive baseball games played for the Baltimore Orioles. After all, 40 years is over 2,000 Sundays!

One week, in the middle of a worship service, I told Judy I needed her to leave the room. It was an awkward moment, but she complied, and I shared the idea of the church bells with the congregation. They have loved Judy and her family since she had been a regular in the youth group, and faces lit up. They agreed that it was a great idea.

They also agreed to keep it a secret. I thought that would be a longshot, but I trusted them.

I polled some of the neighborhood using *Facebook, Twitter,* and *Nextdoor,* and our neighbors were excited about what would instantly become an iconic part of the already iconic neighborhood. We worked on raising money for the bells, which would cost about $15,000. It wasn't easy for the small congregation to pull together that much money, and we were about $6,000 short, but a very generous, long-time member family agreed to donate the remainder, and the installation began.

They were going to be electronic, using massive speakers on the roof to project the sound of the bells over a mile in each direction. I needed the wiring expertise of one of the best people I ever met, Larry Blankenship, to pull it off.

"Larry, I need you to make this, and while you're doing it, you can't let Judy catch you." By that time Larry had become accustomed to strange requests from me, so he looked at the sheet, then back at me with an unfazed smirk. "All right, I can do that." Larry's wife, Carol, and daughter, Deni, were heroic volunteers at Seminole Heights, and between them and our amazing church business administrator, Sarah Ellis, there were enough people around to keep watch for any unexpected appearances by Judy, so he pulled it off. (Those four helped hold that building and congregation together for me at times when I could not seem to find a way, and this book won't be long enough to do justice to the often varied and sometimes odd ways they came through for me, but the clandestine bell installation is a pretty good example.)

By the time the Sunday came to celebrate Judy's many years of service, thousands of our neighbors had been surveyed about the bells, and hundreds of church members had known about them for almost a year. Miraculously, Judy had no idea.

After worship one Sunday, we had a special presentation outside. We set up chairs around the north side steps, where we unveiled a plaque that thanked her for her many years of faithful service, and dedicated to her the "Judy Colvin Chimes."

I read the plaque out loud, and as I did, she thought I was talking about the handbells used by our handbell choir. That would have been appropriate, as she had led the handbell choir for most of those 40 years. People began clapping, and she did too. After that, Judy, our congregation, and everybody else within about a mile-and-a-half of the church finally got to hear the Judy Colvin Chimes. She stopped clapping, looked up into the sky, and realized I wasn't talking about the handbells. It is and will always be one of my favorite moments of my ministry career.

We conversed with the neighborhood using social media, as well as the principal at the school next door, about the best daily schedule for the bells. They rang on the hour from 3 p.m. until 8 p.m. Monday–Friday (so they wouldn't ring until after school), and from noon until 8 p.m. on weekends. There was a special low toll for the end of a funeral, and a celebratory ring for weddings and other joyous occasions. We rang them for the students next door at times like the start of Christmas break and Summer vacation. During Advent, we'd play a Christmas carol or hymn (some sacred, some secular) on the bells each day at 5 p.m., adding to the spirit of the season in the neighborhood.

Whenever we planned to ring the bells, we'd put out a notice on social media; letting the neighborhood know the reason. These turned into online opportunities for neighbors outside the church to express condolences for funerals, congratulations for weddings, and well wishes for kids to have a good summer. Overnight the sound of the bells from Seminole Heights United Methodist became a treasured element of the neighborhood's atmosphere.

Seminole Heights United

I WAS ABOUT TO do a sermon series on Moses, and I found out that a member at Hyde Park United Methodist had made a really cool life-sized replica of the Ark of the Covenant for a series they'd done. It was stored away in a basement at Hyde Park's Downtown "Portico" Campus, just sitting there unused, much like it was in the last scene of *Raiders of the Lost Ark*.

I made some calls, and got permission to borrow it. I was driving a 2007 Nissan Altima at the time, which had decent trunk space, but not Ark of the Covenant-sized trunk space. So I made a call to Brian Frey.

Brian became a good friend during my time at Seminole Heights. He had been a member at a large United Methodist church in Atlanta before moving to Tampa with his husband, Troy. I first met them during a neighborhood home tour event, when we opened up the church to people to come by and see our historic space as they walked around to have a look at the many early 20th century bungalows that are the standard style house in the area.

We discussed the pipe organ, because he'd been on a committee to have work done on the organ at his church in Atlanta and knew a lot more about it than I did. Beyond that, I quickly found Brian to be someone who is intimately acquainted with the underbelly of church committee life. He spoke my language, and easily made several accurate guesses about the oddities of my life as the pastor at Seminole Heights.

Brian has many years of professional experience in theater set and lighting design, and later on agreed to revamp our entire Christmas decoration look, which blew everybody away. It was a massive upgrade, without a single complaint from anyone about the pitfalls of change. Anyone who has ever worked at a church knows that's a Christmas miracle in itself.

Fortunately for me, on the day I got permission to borrow the Ark of the Covenant, Brian and his pickup truck were available to help. It was a funny phone conversation.

"Hey Brian, do you have time this week to help me pick something up and bring it to the church in your truck?"

"Yeah, I think so," he replied, "What are we getting?"

"The Ark of the Covenant."

Pause. "Where'd you find it?"

"Would you believe Hyde Park United Methodist, right here in Tampa?"

"Always the last place you look."

When we got it loaded into the bed of his truck, I had an idea. "You know what would be funny? Let me get a video of you casually driving by with the Ark of the Covenant in the back of your truck."

"All right, let's do it."

Now, what would have been smart would have been to some-how secure the Ark of the Covenant, maybe with some bungee cords or something, but that didn't occur to us. So, Brian slowly rolled the truck into the frame from the right, and out on the left. He then continued another 7–10 feet and stopped to let me get back in, at which point the unsecured Ark of the Covenant slid forward in the truck bed, crashing into the cab of the truck and breaking a wing off of one of the cherubs on top of the carefully rendered replica. My mouth gaped open in horror. Brian didn't see the damage right away, but he saw my face.

"Is it bad?"

Fortunately for me, Brian's husband, who can repair just about anything, was also available to help. Rather than heading to the church, we detoured to Brian and Troy's. I called while Brian drove.

"Hey Troy, it's Matt Horan. Listen, I'm with Brian, and, well, we just broke the Ark of the Covenant, and we're coming in hot. Do you think you can fix it?"

Pause. "You broke the Ark of the Covenant?"

"Correct."

"And you're bringing it here?"

"Well, if it's any consolation, it's not the real one, or else we would probably have been struck by lightning and killed by now." (See 2 Samuel 6:6–7)

Thanks to his amazing craftsmanship, the broken wing was unnoticeable, and went on display as planned that Sunday. (If anyone from Hyde Park reads this—sorry about that wing.)

Brian was an enormous help in expanding my vision for Seminole Heights to become the neighborhood's church. He was the president of a nearby neighborhood association, and we began hosting their monthly meetings in our fellowship hall. It was a gathering of about 30–40 people, and they were all a great group that I enjoyed getting to know.

Amber and Robb were two more heroic leaders at Seminole Heights, and I'm not sure what I would have done without their partnership and friendship. Among other things, they were the Christmas tree lot czars for four out of my five years there. (I reluctantly gave them a year off when they were out of the country.)

Robb had an idea one day that really seemed like the next stage in growing the impact of the church. The idea was to create a church membership for people who wanted to be a part of the community service work of the church, but weren't really interested in the "spiritual stuff." He predicted that there would be plenty of people who would believe in the mission to be good neighbors whether they were followers of Jesus or not. I floated the idea in a couple of online groups, and a lot of people thought it had promise. One person posted that you could just lop off the

"Methodist Church" from the name, and call this service arm of the church "Seminole Heights United." We gasped at the sound of it. That was perfect.

In fact, we had no idea how perfect the idea was, as one day it just started happening by itself. It got underway with someone in the neighborhood posting a nice message on the church's *Facebook* page: "You know, there is so much that you guys do for this community. Is there anything we can do for you?"

I guess I was in a sarcastic mood that night, because I went on a long listing spree in response, naming all of the many things in or around our buildings that needed long overdue repairs or attention. I honestly shared the list in jest, following it up with, "In all seriousness that's an incredibly kind offer! Let me think on it for a day or two and get back to you."

They ended up not giving me a day or two. In fact, what happened next was a turning point in the church's relationship with our neighborhood.

One by one people began posting responses to my list and started claiming the various items on it. One woman spent about a week organizing our attic, which had been a hot mess full of about 50 years of storage. People took shifts pressure washing the sidewalks and side walls of the church building. Two guys came and reorganized the spider web of wires going from our sound system to the platform in front of the sanctuary. A woman came and gave the side of our preschool building a long-overdue landscaping makeover. Someone came and organized our maintenance supply closet, which hadn't been done since we last had a staff maintenance person over a decade before, and he replaced the light ballast so that the light could turn on in there for the first time in ages. A guy came and resurrected a sprinkler system under the church property that I didn't even know existed.

Then, a group that had been working on various beautification projects in the neighborhood received a grant for us to have a brand new landscaped garden planted in front of the church. Some landscape architects and about 20 volunteers—half from the church and half neighbors who just wanted to help—showed up on a Saturday morning and transformed the walk up to our front steps with native plants and a drip irrigation system. After we finished installing the garden, our lay leaders had an emergency meeting, because Seminole Heights United was happening right before our eyes and we needed to get the ball rolling on making it a sustained reality.

We pulled together a board of directors for Seminole Heights United, and it was a phenomenal team. It included Amber and Robb, Brian, another local neighborhood association president named Stan, the former police chief of Tampa and future mayor, Jane Castor, Tiffany, an amazing school psychologist at Memorial Middle School, and some awesome neighbors named Johanna and Ellie.

Our first order of business was to begin work on a plan to partner with the middle school. Memorial had been cited as an underperforming school several years in a row, and was under pressure to improve or else they'd be taken over by the Florida Department of Education. We began casting vision for the entire neighborhood to adopt Memorial by donating supplies, attending their sporting events and arts performances, offering tutoring, providing translation help for its many Spanish-speaking students, updating the sound system in their gym, and doing a makeover for the teachers' lounge.

It didn't take long for the volunteers and supplies to start rolling in. The church set aside the money to pay for the sound system upgrade in our neighborhood partnerships budget. They invited the board members to their first pep rally with the new sound system, which was *electric* after years of not being able to hear any words said or songs played in the gym before!

The teachers and administrators at the school had heard a lot of promises before, but hadn't always seen the promises kept. This group, however, understood that a neighborhood rises and falls with its schools; affecting everything from property values to businesses moving in. More than that, as residents got a look at how much Tiffany and the teachers cared about the kids and were working triple-time to help them succeed, they simply started inspiring us.

The Murder of Anthony Naiboa

JUST A MONTH BEFORE Benjamin Mitchell was murdered, Hurricane Irma hit Tampa. It caused significant damage to many structures in the area, and resulted in residents gathering up large piles of leaves and branches that had fallen along the streets. City of Tampa workers made herculean efforts to try and clear out the gathered heaps of debris, but there were still plenty left a month later. Some theorized that the piles created hiding places to conceal the Seminole Heights serial killer before and after his murders, making it easier to surprise victims and harder to catch him afterwards, but it's unclear whether or not they were a factor in either.

While Irma brought plenty of rain and wind to Tampa as a Category 2, it was a Category 5 hurricane when it first made landfall in the United States, hitting the island of Puerto Rico with 185 mile-per-hour winds. It was followed by a similar sized storm, Hurricane Maria, just a couple weeks later. They did unfathomable damage to the small island, requiring a logistically challenging relief effort made even more difficult by political animus between local and federal governments.

Many families in the Tampa Bay Area have close ties to friends and family in Puerto Rico, and so it did not take long for people to watch the uneven response and begin taking matters into their own hands. Faith communities and other groups collected supplies to send to the decimated American territory, and they were collected in warehouses around the Tampa Bay Area for sorting and shipping. One warehouse in Tampa employed 20-year-old Anthony Naiboa.

Anthony was diagnosed early on with autism. He was high-functioning, and decided in high school that he did not want to get a special diploma with lower academic standards. So, he buckled down and fought hard through school to get a real diploma, becoming a favorite of his teachers and administrators in the process. He then interviewed for jobs over 20 times, and was laid off once before finally getting the job at the warehouse. He was proud to start taking responsibility for some of his expenses, and after he got his first paycheck he insisted on taking his family out to dinner. When the check came, he reached out, put his hand on top of it, looked at his family with a smile and proudly said, "I got this."

October 19th was a Thursday, six days after city workers discovered Monica Hoffa's body and two days after Chief Dugan's announcement about the weapon that connected the two murders. At 7:26 p.m., Anthony called his family to say that the schedule had changed and he was taking a different bus home than usual. He was let out on 15th Street, and he began walking north in the direction of the bus stop where Benjamin Mitchell died eleven days earlier.

Around 7:55 p.m., Anthony's walk north brought him within view of the bus stop where Mitchell was killed. He usually looked down at his feet while he walked, but if he looked up at all he would have been able to see the makeshift memorial of flowers and stuffed animals that had been accumulating there.

Donaldson began to approach him from behind. In a coincidence that seems almost too impossible to fathom, Anthony's walk took him in front of Benjamin Mitchell's house, and it was there that Donaldson closed to within arm's reach, firing a bullet into the back of Anthony's head, killing him instantly.

Police officers patrolling the neighborhood, already on heightened alert, heard the gunshot. Knowing the killer could be close, every spare unit was called in to try and seal off the area. A police helicopter arrived, and a K-9 unit was brought in to try and capture the killer's scent. They scanned the streets looking for anyone running from the scene, or perhaps anyone matching the individual from the Frierson St. video, but despite the rush of resources just moments after the shot was fired, the Seminole Heights serial killer vanished for the third time in eleven days.

When we woke up the following morning to start our carpool routine, I had a short text message waiting for me from Brian. *"It happened again."*

Three separate murders in eleven days by the same person. Seminole Heights had a serial killer.

"Bring Me His Head"

THE FIRST TWO MURDERS were concerning to everyone, but the murder of Anthony Naiboa seemed to paralyze neighborhood. The usually flourishing restaurants, bars, coffee shops, and other businesses were suddenly empty every night. The once busy sidewalks no longer had any dog walkers, joggers, bike riders, or families going for a stroll together after dinner. Social media posts on *Facebook*, *Nextdoor*, and *Twitter* that were normally full of recommendations, suggestions, and reviews of neighborhood businesses and experiences now contained little more than theories about who it could be and how they kept getting away.

Beyond that, the Seminole Heights serial killer was now a national news story. Brian and Stan were interviewed repeatedly by local and national news outlets as people across the country got to know what the neighborhood was normally like, and what it was like now that its residents were in grave danger.

To their credit, both of them did a great job in interviews *not* making the story about the murderer. Reporters wanted grim quotes about fear and distress, but what they got from Brian and Stan were quotes about our people, about their care for one another, about the resilience that would see us through, and about the amazing response and presence of the Tampa Police Department and other Bay Area law enforcement agencies who were hard at work to find the killer.

Back in 2010, there was an election for mayor of Tampa. I'd only been there a couple years at that point, and so I didn't really know much about the people that were running. I attended a debate between the candidates at a local Catholic church, and got there pretty early for some reason, so I had the chance to observe the candidates arrive. There were places set up on a stage for five candidates, each with a name placard indicating who would be sitting where, and a moderator. The spot in the middle was for the one I figured was probably the favorite, who had actually been mayor of Tampa before. The ones to his left and right I recognized, as well as the one on the end on the right side. I didn't recognize the name on the left end—Bob Buckhorn.

He took his place first, chatting briefly with someone who seemed to be an assistant, and then sat there by himself waiting for the debate to begin. Three non-front runners arrived and seemed to know people (and each other) and did some hobnobbing before taking their seats. A person who seemed to be coordinating the event stopped and chatted briefly with the three of them, seeming to know them, and then made a pleasant but all-business check in with Buckhorn. I didn't get the impression they knew each other, nor did the coordinator seem all that interested in getting to know him. I guess that was the life of a long shot—stuck on the very end on the debate stage, trying to get a little oxygen if the front-runners left some for anybody else.

As the moderator began welcoming everyone, the elephant in the room was that the former—and favored to be the future—mayor wasn't there. I wondered if he felt that his name recognition was so great that he didn't really need a debate, but he walked in a couple minutes later, apologizing for being late. I expected that I'd be impressed with him and probably vote for him since he'd done the job before, but being late to the debate was unimpressive.

When he got the first question, he seemed unprepared. He dropped a lot of names of people he knew that would be helping him, but the impression I took away from him was that debating was nice and all, but he and everybody already knew that he was going to win. The other candidates were prepared, and gave well-informed and nuanced answers that demonstrated that they knew the City of Tampa and what it was facing.

Buckhorn was the last one to answer. The front runner lost me, I already had a new favorite from among the other three based on the first question, and by the time it came to the guy I'd never heard of before, I was nervous for him, quietly rooting for him to not embarrass himself. As he responded, however, Scripture came to mind, from Luke 6:45:

"It is from the overflow of the heart that the mouth speaks."

Everyone had given answers out of the considerable volume of knowledge in their heads in order to convince people to vote for them, but his guy—he knew the same things everybody else did, but seemed to talk less to win people over and more because he might explode if he didn't. After his first answer, I decided that I'd vote for him, even though he probably wasn't going to win. By the end of the debate, I was pretty disappointed he wasn't going to win. It seemed like he'd be an awesome mayor.

Eventually, I discovered I'm a pretty terrible election forecaster, because once the votes were counted, Bob Buckhorn became the 58th Mayor of the City of Tampa.

It's not every elected official that gets a "bullhorn moment" like George W. Bush had at Ground Zero after the September 11th attacks, but Bob Buckhorn had one during the hunt for the Seminole Heights serial killer. He was involved every day, and you could see that he took it personally that someone would terrorize his city in the way this killer had.

The third victim, Anthony Naiboa, was killed on Thursday, October 19th. A few days later, as officers gathered for a roll call with Chief Dugan in a Seminole Heights park to begin their shift patrolling the neighborhood, Buckhorn showed up and gave them a pep talk. He spoke from the overflow of his heart as usual, thanking them for their extra hours and vigilance, and then concluded, "Bring his head to me, all right? Let's get it done."

As a pastor and servant of the Prince of Peace Himself, I had mixed emotions about the idea of the killer's head being brought to the mayor, but the effect it had on the neighborhood could not be denied. "Bring his head to me" t-shirts started showing up. El-lie from the Seminole Heights United board made t-shirts that said, "We Are Seminole Heights," and she couldn't make them fast enough. A group called the Guardian Angels, uniformed volunteers in white shirts and unmistakable red berets who take shifts walking the streets of dangerous neighborhoods, showed up and spent time every night adding their presence to the many police officers pushing back against the serial killer.

For many, Buckhorn's words seemed to shift the feeling in the neighborhood. Before, the focus had been staying inside and staying safe, but more and more, people wanted to do something. The congregation at Seminole Heights United Methodist was about to get their chance.

"I May Know A Guy"

A COUPLE DAYS AFTER Anthony Naiboa was killed, I stayed a little longer after a committee meeting ended to get a few things done. I was about to call Susan, because she wanted to come and pick me up in the car rather than letting me take my usual two-block walk home with a serial killer still at large. Brian popped into my office to say hello, as his neighborhood association meeting had just ended. I asked him if he minded giving me a two-block ride home to save my wife the trip, and once I assured him we wouldn't be hauling any ancient Biblical artifacts, he agreed.

He then said that he was planning to meet up with some people at Ella's, home of the stuffed two-headed alligator I mentioned in the preface. I was tired, but he made the pitch that we needed to keep supporting all of our struggling local businesses, so it was my *responsibility* to go. He's very persuasive.

So, I let Susan off the hook for the two-block ride home, and headed to Ella's with Brian.

We saw Stan sitting in an outdoor booth with one other person and room for two more, and he waved us over. We sat down, and realized that the person he was sitting with was Robert Hoffa, uncle of Monica Hoffa, the second murder victim. My pastor instincts kicked on and I shifted into consoling mode, expecting to find them deep in conversation about the loss of their niece and neighbor, but that wouldn't be necessary.

Robert looked at me and, much to Brian and Stan's amusement, said "Father Matt!" There was no consoling happening. These were friends out for a drink, or in Robert's case, maybe two. I did make an effort to explain that United Methodist pastors don't go by "Father," and that it was really fine to just call me Matt.

"You mean you don't have the shirt with the collar and all that?"

"Well, yeah," I admitted, "I do have one of those, but I don't wear it that often."

"You should wear it tonight!" he suggested.

"I should wear it out drinking with my friends?" I don't actually drink very often, but that wasn't an important distinction to make in the moment.

He leaned in and grinned, "Might make people behave themselves a little better."

That made me laugh. "Would it work on you, you think?"

"Unlikely," Stan added.

He leaned in lower, his grin turned mischievous, and he reached out to shake my hand to congratulate me for my sense of humor with a drawn out, "Father Maaaaatt, ha ha ha!"

I'd met Robert before briefly, but getting to hang out with him that night, someone who had known and loved one of the victims her whole life, was an unexpected gift to me. Stan and Brian had spent time with many of the victims' family members, but I hadn't. It took the ordeal out of the realm of news stories and community leadership tasks, and made it far more personal. From getting to know and laugh with him, I had a feeling Monica would have been fun to hang out with too.

It had been scary to think about the murders, and worrisome to wonder when it would happen again. That night, however, it became more than that. It became profoundly sad.

In the days following Anthony's murder, Stan had a few conversations with Casimar Naiboa, Anthony's father. He learned that they didn't have a church, and didn't have a place to have the funeral. Stan told him, "Hang on, I may know a guy."

On Stan's end of the call, I hope I sounded competent and confident as I agreed to have Anthony's funeral at Seminole Heights. On my end, my eyes went so wide I'm glad they didn't fall right out of my head. Of course, I wanted Seminole Heights to be a church that people turned to in times of need. I wanted us to be the neighborhood's church. I wanted to be able to do things like this whenever they were needed, and do them well; but I wasn't sure we were ready.

First, this would be a very, very public event, covered by the *national* news media, and I had exactly two full time staff members other than me, one of which ran the preschool. The other one, our office manager, Paige, was 24-years-old, but looked about 15. Could she boss reporters around and get them to stay where they were supposed to be and keep them from getting in the way?

> Relationships with neighborhood associations were important.

Second, Anthony Naiboa was black. As far as our diversity went, Seminole Heights United Methodist had exactly one black member. His name is Ronnie—a super guy, but not nearly enough to change the fact that Seminole Heights' congregation is very, very white. When I was in seminary, I'd been an intern as a hospital chaplain, and when I'd seen black families grieve a tragic loss like this, it was in a far more expressive, emotional way than I'd ever seen with the family of a white person. How would volunteers from our church respond? What if there was screaming? What if someone falls to the ground in anguish? What if someone cries out in agony and anger at God? Could Seminole Heights United Methodist handle it?

The Lost Soles

I MET WITH ANTHONY's family a couple days later. They were totally lost as far as how to plan a funeral, and they'd just learned that Brian received a donation from someone in the neighborhood to give a pre-paid burial plot for Anthony. They had questions about what happens at a funeral, and about the difference between that and what happens at a cemetery. They knew there should be some songs at some point, and that someone should talk. They so badly just wanted to stop and cry at times, but they felt a burden to do these things well for Anthony and all the people who would be there.

It was a great privilege to walk with them through it. We designed services for both that would help people grieve and celebrate Anthony. We picked out some church songs, but added *Try Everything* by Shakira as well. Having the details ironed out gave them a lot of peace.

While I sat with Casimar, Anthony's father, he was naturally awash in sadness. My role is to offer a ministry of presence, rather than doing things to get him to feel better, but this time I felt a great desire to just give him a brief sadness reprieve.

I've played soccer since I was six years old. I played through high school, and then on my college fraternity's intramural team. After that I coached soccer at the school where I taught. When we moved to Tampa, I coached my kids' teams, and I signed up to play in an adult league for people too old to be that good anymore, but not old enough to give up the habit quite yet. I've been involved with soccer in one form or another for most of my life.

I got a phone call after I first signed up with the Tampa Bay Club Sport league, informing me that I had been assigned to play on a team called the "Lost Soles." The irony was not lost on me that a church pastor was going to be playing for the Lost Soles (even though it is "Soles," as in the bottom of your shoes). My teammates have enjoyed the irony as well. In fact, I've been on this team for about seven years, and they've all become treasured friends.

So my idea to give him a sadness break was to invite him to play soccer with the Lost Soles at our next game. He said he'd love to, but that he didn't have the cleats, socks, shin guards, etc. I told him not to worry about it, as surely the team could come up with stuff he could borrow. He was excited to join us, and planned on coming out for our next game.

A problem arose when I asked him his shoe size. Turns out he wears size 13. Now, if you know soccer, you know that it's rare to find a soccer player with size 13 feet. I'm not sure why—maybe by the time their feet get that big a swim coach somewhere convinces them to put their flippers to better use in the pool.

I sent a message to my team and let them know that I had invited Casimar to play with us. They'd all been following the story of the Seminole Heights serial killer, and were glad to welcome him. A few players even expressed how honored they were to be a part of my ministry with Anthony's dad. However, glad and honored as

> Whether they're a part of the church or not, people will gladly participate in the good churches do.

they were, none of them wore size 13 cleats. I asked around everywhere I could, but even shoe stores didn't seem to carry cleats in stock that big.

I tried looking for some at a *Play-it-Again Sports*, scanning through every pair of the used shoes they had on their shelves, but there was nothing close to a 13. I was walking out of the store when an employee asked if he could help me find anything. I told him I was looking for size 13 cleats, but that they didn't have any. Then there was a miracle.

"Wait," he said, caught off guard by my request, "Someone just walked in two minutes ago and sold us a pair of size 13 cleats. They've never even been used."

Now, anyone who knows me knows that I am slow to claim that something is a "miracle." It's just too easy to get sucked into a debate with somebody who wants to explain how it could be a coincidence. So I usually prefer to just be thankful for fortuitous circumstances without feeling a need to call it a miracle, but in this case, I mean, *come on!*

I walked out of there paying twenty bucks for a brand new pair of size 13 cleats that would usually go for about ninety. In hindsight, I probably should have run out of the store to see if I could catch up to Jesus before he got in his car and drove off to his next miracle. It would be interesting to see what kind of car he drove. Probably something sensible.

Casimar was warmly welcomed by the team. After finding his miracle shoes, I wondered if God was going to let him score eight goals for us or something to encourage him further, but apparently the miracle stopped at the shoes. The goals didn't materialize, but he didn't stop smiling the whole time, and that was more than enough for me.

I was just so proud after that game. I don't even remember if we won, but I was proud of Casimar for getting out and having some fun, proud of my team for helping me love this hurting family, and proud of Jesus for dropping off those shoes just in time.

October

THE MONTH OF OCTOBER that year gave Seminole Heights United Methodist the chance to see what we were made of. I stopped letting youth group kids walk home from the church, and we made sure nobody walked out to their car by themselves at night. We tried to make sure we scheduled events during the day as much as possible, but unfortunately, we had an event that ended after dark every night during the month of October—the pumpkin patch.

We made the decision to close the patch each night a little earlier so that the volunteers would not be out there too long into the evening. We increased the minimum number of volunteers present in the last shift from two to three, so that there was never anyone out there by themselves if someone had to go inside for a bathroom break. While some shifts were hard to fill, we were able to boost our volunteer base by inviting SHU friends to help out, as well as by offering a chance for local high school students to earn social service hours they needed for club memberships or to add to college scholarship applications. (It didn't count as "religious service" because proceeds from the pumpkin patch

> We told high school guidance counselors about our events at which students could earn community service hours.

funded our school partnerships with our preschool, Seminole Heights Elementary, and Memorial Middle School.)

The congregation always showed up big for unloading when our semi-truck of pumpkins arrived, and over the course of three or four hours, an orange wonderland would come together. It was well lit and designed to create photogenic spots throughout. Every day during school, classes would take field trips from our preschool, Seminole Heights Elementary, and other schools in the area for story time in the pumpkin patch, and for students to pick out their own mini pumpkin. There were crazy looking gourds, as well as thousands of orange pumpkins with some white and green ones as well. A lot of babies smiled for a lot of pictures in there, and it gave young families a safe place to go to get out of the house where they knew there'd be lots of people around. And we were an *Instagram* sensation!

One of the looming uncertainties from having a serial killer in the neighborhood was whether or not anyone would take their kids out trick-or-treating on Halloween. A couple weeks before, Mayor Buckhorn and Chief Dugan said that they'd personally be out trick-or-treating with the kids and families of Seminole Heights, and that the many officers committed to the search for the shooter would be out on the streets making sure that it was safe.

For us, we wondered if we should hold our annual "trunk-or-treat" event. Every year on Halloween, church members parked their cars in a circle around the parking lot, decorated them with the theme of their choice, and then gave out candy to kids who would come through. We then had games and contests, and created a mini-pumpkin patch area in which kids could bring blankets and chairs and sit and watch the Peanuts' *It's the Great Pumpkin, Charlie Brown* movie. Conceivably, we could be an entire Halloween in one stop for those little trick-or-treaters who might not have the endurance for the whole neighborhood.

We debated the wisdom of possibly gathering many potential targets into one small space, and decided that, as long as we could find an off-duty police officer to be present and park their car out front with the lights flashing, we'd do it, because the neighborhood needed it. However, there were not many off-duty police officers to be found that night! When we got word that our request could not be filled, I called my emergency backup, former Chief Jane, to see if she had any ideas. I'm not sure what she did, but there was a police officer at our trunk-or-treat with lights flashing, and hundreds of neighbors came by, thankful for the opportunity, the safety, and the candy.

The Funeral of Anthony Naiboa

OF COURSE, OUR BIGGEST test in October of 2017 was Anthony Naiboa's funeral. We had to be a little picky about who could volunteer for that, because there would be theological communication involved, and we needed to take responsibility for what would be said. It would not be helpful for a volunteer to suggest reasons to a grieving friend or family member for "why" this happened. God didn't need another angel in heaven. God didn't need Anthony to be murdered to get the media to come to a funeral so that they'd end up broadcasting something from the Bible, and everything doesn't happen for a reason; but I could only ensure that those things would not be said to grieving friends and family members if I had the chance to give some orientation to the people who might find themselves in those conversations ahead of time.

So I was able to communicate, both in person and in writing, some instructions to our volunteers. I asked them to simply be like Jesus. Just as Jesus came to be present with us, now we would be present with others in their time of need. They were charged to listen, to be fully present if someone began to share something with them, and to feel no responsibility at all to give answers or explanations. While we did have some people from SHU who helped out a little, this one mostly fell on the congregation, and they did not let me down.

We were very intentional about staffing the parts that we really couldn't get wrong. I gave Paige, our office manager, authority to boss the media around, and she did so, but with a helpful and graceful spirit. She worked with the media relations director for the Tampa Police Department, and he sent an advance list of requirements and instructions to news outlets days before the service, so they knew what to expect before they arrived. She got them all set up in the balcony long before people began arriving for the service so they wouldn't be in the way, and had our worship band leader get them a direct audio feed from the pulpit so that there wouldn't be 15 microphones set up on it like the podium at a news conference. Finally, she kept them from coming down to try and interview people at inappropriate moments, taking requests from them to ask specific people for interviews if they were willing afterward. To their (and Paige's) credit, most people didn't even notice they were there during the service, and thanks to them, the service was broadcast on TV and their web sites. I think I saw that someone was watching from as far away as Sweden.

The biggest job was for the volunteers who would sit with Anthony's family and escort them around the building. We didn't want them to get stuck talking to everybody as they came in or went out, so we set up rooms for them where they could arrive first and sit together away from everybody else. Those were Amber, hero of the Christmas tree lot, who is a college professor at the University of South Florida (USF) and an expert on emotional traumas; and another church member named Dani, who runs a program for victims of sexual abuse, also at USF. Beyond their expertise, they both had the right spirit for the job, and I was so thankful to have their many gifts as a resource for Anthony's family.

Another concern we had was for security. As I write, Donaldson is in custody awaiting trial with a mountain of information about him and the murders now readily available for anyone to look up—including the lack of any established link between the victims that made them his targets. At the time, however, we didn't know anything about who the shooter was or why he was killing people. We didn't know of any connections between Benjamin,

Monica, or Anthony then, but that didn't mean that one still couldn't surface at some point. Other than having seen a couple brief security camera clips in the news that may or may not have been the murderer, he was a complete mystery to everybody.

Therefore, we were left to wonder what a serial killer was thinking, and whether he might see the funeral as a target. Was there a reason the shooter targeted Anthony? Might he have had a relationship with others among his friends or family, making the funeral a target with all of them assembled together? Assuming his moral compass was askew at best and non-existent at worst, might the chance to have many people gathered at once in the same place make the funeral an enticing place to take his next shots?

> Police officers have seen it all, and gave good advice on what to expect people to do.

I asked Chief Dugan and former Chief Castor their opinion, and both felt it was unlikely. Dugan agreed to station an officer with flashing police cruiser lights in front of the church just in case, keeping an eye on everyone who came and went.

Honestly, I didn't believe the shooter would try to kill anyone at the funeral. There was a large crowd of potential witnesses, and it was in the middle of the day, making it much harder to vanish as usual afterward. Still, I knew that the shooter could walk right in and sit in the service like a regular attender, waiting for the moment of his choice to strike. A police officer outside would still have to get up the front steps and into the building before being able to intervene. I admit, this all seems paranoid now. I guess these are just the things that run through your head when there's a serial killer in your neighborhood.

When it comes to the safety of people on my church campus, I don't like to just hope it'll be okay. If their safety is my responsibility, I prefer to actually be responsible. So, we asked a favor from some neighbors. A young couple who had recently moved to the neighborhood were FBI agents. They were friendly and outgoing, buying a house and very quickly doing some skilled landscaping and fixing the place up all by themselves. If you were guessing what they did for a living when you first met them, "FBI agent" would not be one of your first fifty guesses. However, we told them of our concerns about the funeral, and knowing that they were always sufficiently armed for FBI action wherever they went, we asked them to attend, and they did.

God provided one more layer of protection over the funeral when the Guardian Angels, who had been helping patrol the streets of Seminole Heights, all showed up. The group leader offered to have them stationed around the lobby where Anthony's body would be displayed for viewing before the service, just to be an added "presence," as well as to be there if anybody needed anything. I gladly accepted, and I think the greeters at the door were glad for their presence as well, as all of them looked like they could handle themselves if anything was amiss.

Apparently, this was not their first tragic funeral, because that leader knew where his guys needed to be. As groups of Anthony's family and friends were brought to the lobby to see him by Amber and Dani, the Guardian Angels caught multiple people who fell over in anguish, and gently guided them to the ground. I told my volunteers ahead of time that there could be moments of volatile, unfiltered emotion during both the viewing and the funeral, and gave some guidance about how to be present with a person in such a raw state, but there were moments when the mourners outnumbered my volunteers, and they filled right in. I know that sometimes neighborhoods have felt that the Guardian Angels were intrusive or unnecessary, but I have nothing but good things to say about how they served Anthony's family and friends that day.

In the end, Anthony's funeral was a terrible, beautiful event. I was so proud of my congregation for how they served those in attendance, helping them walk from the screams and cries of the viewing, through all the elements of the service, including serving Holy Communion to everyone in attendance. When it was over, we reopened the casket for people to have one last chance to say goodbye, but the atmosphere among his loved ones as they gathered around his body this time was transformed. There were hugs, handshakes, conversations, and above all, *laughter*. We had walked with them from despair to hope, and I could see on the faces of our volunteers afterward that they knew something powerful had transpired in that sanctuary that day. All of us felt honored to have been a part of it.

After lingering for a few moments with Casimar and Maria, I left them with the rest of their family and friends, telling them they could stay as long as they wanted. They took me up on it, staying there together in the front of the sanctuary for about forty-five more minutes, so I walked out through the lobby and out to the porch

> Agreeing to host this big, intimidating event made us get better at hosting big, intimidating events.

at the top of our many front steps. I wanted to reflect for a moment with thanksgiving, because that day Seminole Heights United Methodist had been exactly what I hoped we could be—faithful servants to the neighbors in our community when they needed us.

When I walked out on the porch, I saw three news crews with cameras waiting for people to come out who had agreed to be interviewed. They all had clearly underestimated how long it would be before their interviewees came out, and when I walked out still robed up from the service, all three perked up like they could interview me to grab some backup b-roll footage in case they needed it for their story. However, I was saved by a bell.

These were not our beautiful new church bells, mind you—this was coming from the elevator that takes people from the parking lot to the top of the porch, allowing them to bypass the daunting number of steps you'd have to take. Someone was stuck inside and had pushed the alarm bell.

So I looked to my left at the elevator with people stuck inside, and then looked to my right, where three news crews were now staring at me, probably wondering if it would be tacky to turn their cameras on to capture the sudden drama unfolding in our one-story elevator.

Suppressing the fear I felt that there would be footage of me trying to pry an elevator door open in my clergy robe on the news later that night, I ran for the emergency door handle kept in the lobby. I came running out, jammed the handle into the little hole in the door, and began to push, getting very little traction with my dress shoes on the stone porch floor.

Eventually, I managed to crack the door open, and saw that the car inside had stopped, with the porch floor at chest height of the three twentysomething young men inside. (In case you're wondering, they were all perfectly healthy enough to have taken the stairs.)

One of them had accidentally leaned on the emergency stop switch, and rather than solve the problem themselves by switching it back, rang the emergency bell to call for me to rescue them while a few reporters looked on.

To their credit, none of the reporters turned the cameras in the direction of the elevator. I think I did catch a glimpse of one young intern quickly putting her phone down when I turned back toward them, but I guess I can't really blame her. If they had plunged that one story to their deaths, her phone footage might have been the lead story that night. Fortunately, all three men were able to safely complete the remaining five feet of their elevator ride, and Anthony was able to remain the lead story.

The Murder of Ronald Felton

RONALD FELTON VOLUNTEERED A couple times a week at New Season Apostolic Ministries to serve food to the homeless. He would normally get there around 3 a.m., but because of the shootings he'd started showing up even earlier to wait with people who would begin arriving as early as 1 a.m. for the food pantry that wouldn't open until 7:30 a.m. During the wait he greeted every person who arrived, making sure they felt welcome, and if the wait became too long, he talked them into staying. The early morning of Tuesday, November 14th was no different.

Around 4:15 a.m. he walked over to a laundromat across Nebraska Avenue to use the bathroom. He made a brief call on his cell-phone to his twin brother, Reginald, and then went inside.

There was a group volunteering that day from a well-known Tampa organization that helps people transition out of homelessness, Metropolitan Ministries. They'd been there since about 2:15 a.m., and with the sunrise still a couple hours away, some of them got back into their van to warm up.

One woman with the group sat sideways in the back row of the van, facing a window that looked out at the laundromat. As she settled into her seat, she saw Ronald coming back outside and heading back across the street. Motion in her peripheral vision drew her attention, and she saw a man in black clothes and a baseball cap running toward him. He pointed a gun and fired at

Felton, who instantly fell face down in the middle of the street. The man then stood over him, shot him three more times, and took off running in the direction he came.

With three murders already committed, there were police everywhere. It was less than a minute before officers got to Ronnie. They instinctively scanned for suspects, but unfortunately, everyone in Seminole Heights was on high alert, and once the shots rang out, people ran away in all directions. They quickly put plans in motion to lock down the neighborhood, and in minutes every intersection into or out of the neighborhood was blocked by a police cruiser. The response was so fast and so thorough—surely he wouldn't get away this time. He had to be somewhere within a few blocks of where the shooting took place.

As I drove our carpool toward the corner of Hillsborough and Nebraska that morning, there was no doubt it had happened again. It was as if every emergency vehicle in the Tampa Bay Area had assembled a block south of the intersection.

We drove east on Hillsborough, which was the northern end of the lockdown. Every street on our right was blocked by police. We saw cruisers from the Tampa Police Department, Hillsborough County Sheriff's Department, Florida Highway Patrol, and Florida Department of Law Enforcement. One of the kids in the car was convinced they saw one intersection blocked by officers from Fish and Wildlife. No matter what agency they were from, we didn't see anybody get through those barricaded intersections without law enforcement officers knowing about it.

Not long after we went past, police officers began letting people through for the first time since before 4:30 a.m., but they stopped every car and pedestrian, making note of everyone who came out of or went into the blocked off radius.

The streets in Seminole Heights are a grid, but there are also alleyways that run behind each row of houses. Most of them are not maintained very well, so they provide plenty of potential hiding places. I've wondered if the many alleys crisscrossing the neighborhood gave Donaldson secluded places to park his car, as well as routes out of the area with more tree cover to elude helicopters and repeatedly get away.

The area was scoured with a combination of door-to-door searches of every house, K-9 sweeps of every alley, and overhead scans of every inch of the area by helicopters. Yet despite the quick response time of police officers to the scene and the total lockdown of the area, the Seminole Heights serial killer somehow got away again, leaving nothing behind but a fourth victim, Ronald Felton.

Chief Dugan was alerted to the murder by phone a little before 5 a.m. It was his 51st birthday. From then until just past noon, he was out looking for the killer with a new series of worries. First, the other murders had been in the evening, not too long after dark, but this one happened just before sunrise. The other murders had been committed with care to not be seen, but this one was done with a lot of witnesses standing around. The other murders occurred within a week of each other, but this one was weeks later. The police presence in the neighborhood for the other murders was nothing like what it was this time, but he tried it anyway, and succeeded.

The killer's active time was expanding. He was growing more patient, more brash, and less afraid of the police. It was a recipe to make Dugan wonder if, the next time, police officers would be close enough to become potential victims themselves.

A Moment of Thanksgiving During Two Months of Fear

WE DIDN'T REALIZE IT was possible, but after Ronnie Felton's murder, even more police officers from various departments descended on Seminole Heights. While they tracked down the thousands of leads that came in, the SHU team came up with an idea to show them our appreciation, and to give our eager neighbors something to do as well.

We decided to put on a day long spaghetti lunch and dinner in the church's fellowship hall for all of the law enforcement professionals serving the neighborhood. It would be a way to thank the many men and women working so hard to catch the Seminole Heights serial killer, as well as giving people something to do by volunteering to help put it on.

In the lead up to the event, I told the congregation that this was an "all hands on deck" kind of moment. That's what I often say to counter the assumption, typical in large groups like a church, that someone else will handle a volunteer need, and they don't have to worry about it; but I wanted *everybody* worrying about this one. I expected every single able-bodied human being on our roster to be there and happily help make this happen. We put a call out to our growing SHU roster too, but it was at our place, so I wanted to make sure all bases were covered.

To my amazement, I had to cancel that request shortly after. There has been one time in my 20 years in the employ of the church that I have ever asked my congregation to not volunteer for something—and this was it. We had a response so overwhelming to the call to help with the spaghetti day that I literally had to ask church members to un-volunteer to make room for all of these new volunteers from the neighborhood. The SHU board had to break the day up into relatively short shifts to make room for as many volunteers as possible, and we still had to turn people away. In fact, volunteers who had been turned away showed up all day to help anyway, and we had to put signs up apologizing and thanking people, but saying that if you weren't already booked for a shift, we couldn't work you in.

Countless uniformed first responders poured through our fellowship hall to eat together. Mayor Buckhorn came, as did current Chief Dugan and some of his staff, and former Chief Jane Castor. The highlight was when Kenny Hoffa, Monica Hoffa's dad, drove all the way from South Carolina to surprise the police officers and thank them for all they were doing.

> Serving those who serve others is always time and effort well spent.

Despite the reason for it, I couldn't help but give thanks once again. This was the kind of church I wanted to pastor—one with no delineation between insiders and outsiders, a church that belonged to its neighborhood, who saw our highest and best moments not just as those in which *we* grow in our love for our neighbors, but those in which we bring the whole neighborhood together to love each other. Unfortunately, it's times of crisis that bring those moments about most easily, but I was thankful for the opportunity to see the vision realized right before my eyes nonetheless. After working so hard to give ourselves to our neighborhood for four years, this was the fruit—everyone feeling right at home at Seminole Heights United Methodist.

"He's Under My Porch!"

ONE NIGHT WE THOUGHT they had him.

We had just finished cleaning up from dinner. The girls had a few friends over at the parsonage, so there was a little more noise than usual, but we eventually heard the familiar sound of a police helicopter nearby. It had become so commonplace that when we did hear it, we barely even noticed. This time, however, it was close. *Really* close.

I went outside to see where it was, to which Susan wisely protested, "You know, if it's nearby, maybe there's a serial killer nearby too."

That was a good point. So, I just cracked the door a little, and that was enough to see that the helicopter was over the church campus. I mentally ran through our calendar of events, and was relieved to recall that there was nothing happening at the church that night. The pumpkin patch had ended on Halloween, and the Christmas tree lot was still a couple weeks away.

It was slowly moving northeast, in the direction of the parsonage, and then sped up as it went right over the house. Susan checked the *Nextdoor* app and saw that people on streets right around us were posting that police were chasing somebody on foot through their backyards! I took a look, and was disturbed to see the names of the streets, just two or three blocks north of us. We checked the locks on the doors and closed the blinds on the windows as more and more police cruisers zoomed up Central Avenue past our front door with sirens blaring. Then we just sat together and watched the drama unfold on *Nextdoor* as our neighbors posted a flurry of updates.

"A police car just drove down our back alley!"

"The police chopper is right over our street looking for somebody with their searchlight!"

"Someone just ran through our backyard!"

"Police cars just went racing down our street!"

We could hear the sirens from every direction. It had to be him.

The posts on *Nextdoor* continued, and then one said, "Someone just ran up to our house and crawled under our front porch!"

I couldn't imagine the terror of having the Seminole Heights serial killer under your porch. Just about every house in the neighborhood had a crawl space underneath, and if he got under your porch, he could get underneath just about any part of your house.

We waited and waited for news that the killer had been caught and the ordeal was over, hoping no one would be hurt in the process, but the news never came.

We eventually learned that there was a carjacking elsewhere in Tampa, and as the carjacker fled, he chose the absolute worst place to drive a stolen car—right into a neighborhood crawling with police officers looking for a serial killer. Jane confirmed to us later, "It wasn't the killer, but it might have been the world's worst carjacker."

The McDonald's Salad Bag

TAMPA POLICE DEPARTMENT OFFICER Randy Whitney was one of the hundreds and hundreds of officers who lived on high alert while patrolling the area in or around Seminole Heights in the fall of 2017. She was on a lunch break during her shift on Tuesday, November 28th, and stopped in at a McDonald's in the nearby Ybor City area, just east of Seminole Heights. It had now been 51 days since Benjamin Mitchell's murder.

While she was eating, McDonald's shift manager Yolanda Walker approached her. Officer Whitney could tell right away that she was anxious about something, but all Walker asked her was about whether or not she would be staying at the restaurant for a while. She assured her that she could, but then pressed her about what was the matter. The longer they talked, the more fearful Walker seemed, and eventually Whitney was able to convince her to tell her what was wrong.

She took her to the office in the back, opened a desk drawer, and produced a McDonald's salad bag. Walker told Whitney that a little while ago, one of her employees came in and told her that he needed an advance on his paycheck, because he needed to buy a plane ticket and get out of town for a while. When they looked at how much his paycheck was going to be, it wasn't enough.

Walker recommended a business nearby where he might be able to get a small loan or cash advance, and he went. Before leaving, he handed her the bag, and said he needed her to hold it for him until he got back, telling her not to look inside. She didn't look, but she was pretty convinced that the bag contained a gun.

Her suspicion about what was in the bag suddenly made a few different things come together for her. He had the same build as the guy in the surveillance videos of the Seminole Heights serial killer. He had been acting strangely lately, barely displaying much of any personality at all. In fact, a couple times the other employees had joked that he was so strange—maybe he *was* the guy! The gun in the bag turned the joke into a real and terrifying possibility.

Officer Whitney used a fingernail to pull back the opening of the bag to look inside, and saw the trigger. She then put on gloves, and took out a Glock .40mm handgun, the same kind of gun that had been used in the murders. She would definitely not be leaving that McDonald's any time soon.

She called the discovery in, and other officers headed her way. The first to arrive was Captain Michael Stout, who pulled into the parking lot just as a young man in a McDonald's uniform was getting out of a red car and walking toward the restaurant. Aware of Yolanda Walker's story, he knew that this could be the employee that gave her the gun, and if he was the killer, there was no way he could let him get back inside the restaurant where his gun was. Stout drove his cruiser in-between the employee and the building, got out of the car, aimed his gun, and told him to get down on the ground.

The man at which Captain Stout was aiming his gun was Trai Donaldson, the Seminole Heights serial killer.

Church Bells at Midnight

A COUPLE WEEKS BEFORE the arrest, I made a decision. When the Seminole Heights serial killer was arrested, our church bells at Seminole Heights United Methodist would help spread the news as far as their rings could carry it. We announced on social media that, when the killer was found, we'd ring the bells.

When news of an arrest in the case began to circulate throughout the day on Tuesday, November 28th, we waited for the confirmation to come so we could deliver on the promise. It didn't come during the day, nor before our board of trustees meeting that night. When the meeting ended, I checked news sources, but still didn't see anything. I headed home to grab some dinner, ready to run back to the church if the word became official. I started channel surfing for news around 9:30 p.m., but there was nothing yet, and at that point I began to get cold feet. What if they don't announce it for another hour? Or two? Or three?

I looked at the clock around 9:45 p.m. "Good Lord," I said out loud to my TV, "At this rate I'm going to be ringing the church bells at midnight."

"What?" Jenna was sitting at the dining room table doing homework, still wearing her Blake High School soccer uniform from her game earlier that night.

"Nothing, sorry," I replied. "Just talking to myself." I looked over at her and said, "Thanks for working hard over there," but then I noticed she was hard at work eating a bowl of ice cream. She had a unique way of replenishing her post-game strength.

I texted Jane. She wasn't the police chief anymore, but surely she still knew people.

> **Me:** Hey Jane, Getting nervous about the bells so late. Do they have the guy?
>
> **Jane:** Yeah, but there's more to do before it's official.
>
> **Me:** Ugh. Any idea when? Should I just wait until tomorrow?
>
> **Jane:** Press conference tonight at 11.
>
> **Me:** 11? People with sleeping babies will hate me.
>
> **Jane:** Do it! The neighborhood needs it.
>
> **Me:** Okay. When people complain I'm telling them you talked me into it!
>
> **Jane:** I'm okay with that.
>
> **Matt:** All right. Go outside and listen at 11:01.

Brian texted me not long after. He knew people too.

> **Brian:** They have him. You still ringing the bells?
>
> **Me:** Yeah. I'm nervous about ringing them so late, but Jane says I still should.
>
> **Brian:** Listen to Jane! Do it!

During the 10 p.m. hour, the impending announcement became a less closely guarded secret. A *Facebook* messenger group that started as a way to organize the first responder spaghetti day was alive with commentary—all of them wide awake and rooting for the church bells.

I trusted that they were a decent representative sample of the people that lived within bellshot of the church, most of whom were probably also still awake waiting for the news conference. So, between Jane, Brian, and the spaghetti crew, I gathered enough resolve to risk waking the neighbors.

11 p.m. finally arrived, and I turned on Tampa's News Channel 8. Chief Dugan and Mayor Buckhorn walked up to a podium,

and I tried to read their expressions, but their poker faces were locked in. The Chief began by recounting the names of the victims and the dates of their murders: Benjamin Mitchell on October 9th, Monica Hoffa on October 11th, Anthony Naiboa on October 19th, and Ronald Felton on November 14th. Finally, he said it.

"I am pleased to announce that tonight, we will be making an arrest in the Seminole Heights murders."

I turned off the TV, and walked past Jenna on my way to the door. She looked up at me from scraping the bottom of her ice cream bowl with her spoon. "Where are you going?"

"Gonna go ring the bells."

"Are you serious? Right now?"

"Yeah. Can you let Mommy know where I'm going?"

"Wait! Can I come?"

"No, you need to do your homework," but I had a change of heart in mid-sentence. "No, wait, yes, come on. Someone should record this." (I posted the video of the church with the bells ringing that night on the church's *Facebook* and *Twitter* accounts, and it was shown on the morning news of the local ABC affiliate the next day.)

About 30 seconds later, Susan's phone received a text message from Jenna that said, "Going to church with Daddy." In hindsight, I wasn't very specific about the information I wanted her to convey, but it didn't really matter, because she was in the shower when it arrived and heard the church bells before she got Jenna's message.

Assuming there was some kind of church bell malfunction, she yelled from the shower to alert me, but, of course, got no response. She jumped out of the shower with shampoo still in her hair, threw on a towel, and went looking for me around the house to no avail.

I was sitting in the church office in front of the control console for the bells, listening as they pierced the silence outside when my phone rang. It was Susan.

"Hey, I don't know where you are but it's after 11:00 and the bells are going off."

As you can imagine, my wife was not the only person to notice the bells. Posts on social media from across Seminole Heights said one of four things:

"Are the church bells ringing right now?"

"Anybody know why the church bells are ringing right now?"

"The bells are announcing they caught the Seminole Heights serial killer!"

The fourth option was my favorite: "We saw the news conference, and then heard the church bells, and we all came outside to listen!"

To my surprise, there were no angry social media posts, and only three angry voicemail messages (understandably, all from parents of babies). We got many emails and *Facebook* messages from people thanking us, letting us know how they felt, what they thought and did, and how many of them heard the bells and cried.

Keith Cate is the evening news anchor at News Channel 8, Tampa's NBC affiliate. He and his family have been long time members at Hyde Park United Methodist, where as I mentioned, I'd served as an associate pastor in my first appointment after seminary.

I got to know Keith as he volunteered on a couple different ministry teams and projects with me during my time at Hyde Park. I was honored to officiate at his daughter's wedding, and he once invited me to come to the studio and watch them do the news, which was fascinating. He even let me sit at the desk with him, his co-host, and the weatherman for a picture afterwards. It's one of my all time favorite pictures.

A reporter from News Channel 8 was visiting the church to interview me before trunk-or-treat and get some footage of the area where it would be happening, and he pronounced my name wrong, both live and in the video package. When the segment ended and the camera went back to the news desk, Keith added, "Matt Ho*ran*," saying my name with emphasis to correct the pronunciation "is a good guy doing good work up there," before moving on to the next story. Needless to say, he's my favorite news anchor.

I got back home from ringing the bells in time for the end of the 11:00 news. It seemed that they may have had a few seconds to fill before the end of the last segment, or perhaps they planned for the news team to end the broadcast by talking about their feelings on the capture of the Seminole Heights serial killer. In any event, it was Keith who had the last word before they signed off, and it was a good last word on those scary 51 days in 2017:

"*That's all for us. Jimmy Fallon is up next. Sleep well, Seminole Heights.*"

Why Did You Ring the Bells?

A QUESTION KEPT COMING up the next day from people who'd heard the bells. Sometimes it was by email, and other times in conversation. The question was always framed with thanksgiving, saying that they were glad to have heard the bells that night, but they wanted to know more about church bells and the occasions during which they ring. They assumed they were for the church—the start of a worship service, and for weddings and funerals, because we'd done those before. Of course, they were aware that they also chimed the hour as a public service, but other than that, they're for non-church things too? And if so, why would the capture of a serial killer be a time for church bells to ring?

There was something more underlying these questions that became clear as I heard and read them: *We're not really church people, so why did we feel the way we did when we heard the church bells?* Why would an explosion of sounds suddenly piercing the quiet of the night and echoing across the neighborhood at the end of 51 days of waiting and hoping and hiding and watching and worrying and praying and mourning and searching feel so beautifully resonant within the hearts of the people of Seminole Heights?

I decided to write a post on my blog to answer the question. I sent it to those who had asked, and then posted it for anyone who was wondering. What follows is the post from my blog.

It's probably safe to say that the majority of people in Seminole Heights are not overly enamored with organized religion. Almost 14,000 people live close enough to have heard the bells last night, but Seminole Heights United Methodist—a church with a sanctuary that can hold over 400 people—currently hosts two services each Sunday that average around 40–50 people apiece.

Now there are many reasons for that apart from our neighbors' views on church life, and the vast majority of those reasons are the church's own doing. Regardless of the reasons, it is only the smallest fraction of a percentage of our neighbors that actually attend worship services at Seminole Heights United Methodist. Thus most of what happens in a worship service feels quite foreign, if not funny looking.

It happens in a strangely shaped building, led by a guy in a robe, with music from a pipe organ and a choir of people, also wearing robes. There's odd ceremonies like Holy Communion, baptisms, or Ash Wednesday. And the church bells—certainly out of the ordinary.

Remember back just a couple days ago? I'd stopped walking the two blocks from my house to the church for fear of being shot. The youth group kids that walked to the church from all over the neighborhood now were required to be escorted to and from the church by a parent. Restaurants and businesses were wondering how much longer they could survive with the whole neighborhood hiding at home every night. Benjamin gunned down waiting for a bus. Then Monica. Then Anthony. Then Ronald.

Couldn't you feel it? Couldn't you feel the jarring intrusion of something evil into Seminole Heights? Our extra caution and second glances and heightened suspicion didn't help us see it—it wasn't something you could catch with your senses. You could just feel something that didn't belong lingering in our streets.

That's what evil is. It is a cold, enslaving intrusion into the world that we're never quite prepared for. It sneaks in, striking where we are vulnerable, in hopes of claiming territory that might otherwise have known peace.

Churches are at their best when they are the bearers of the powerful story of Jesus Christ. It's a story of another kind of intrusion—God himself born on a silent night, intruding into the darkness of this world to bring a jarring infusion of light and hope and healing and peace. That is the answer when evil intrudes. Hope must intrude back, reclaiming the territory that evil has seized.

2,000 years later, the church is the legacy left behind by Jesus that continues that tradition of intrusion. For that reason, I walk home every Sunday after church in my clergy collar—getting double takes from people driving by this strange spiritual fashion intrusion of the otherworldly into our world. For that reason I stand out on Central Avenue every Ash Wednesday in my robe and stole, applying ashes to the forehead of anyone who wants to receive them—something normally found inside the church building stepping out as an intrusion of the otherworldly into our world. And so we step outside and have movie nights and pumpkin patches and Christmas tree lots and Trunk-or-Treat and school partnerships and dog park days and Christmas tree lightings and Christmas carols and we refuse to surrender the world to evil and continually look for new ways to intrude and infuse light and hope and peace and love—the otherworldly intruding into this world.

And then, at 11 p.m. on Tuesday night, as the evil hovering over our streets like a dense fog tried once more to settle in and enslave another eerily quiet night in Seminole Heights, the evil recoiled. There was a sudden, jarring, otherworldly musical intrusion of hope and light and joy and peace that shattered the oppressive quiet and staked a claim over the neighborhood that evil had tried to ensnare.

Seminole Heights United Methodist is not a church with big crowds or big budgets. It is a church, however, that will take any opportunity to create the otherworldly intrusions that refuse to allow evil to set up shop in our neighborhood.

That's why you turned the volume down on the TV when you heard them.

That's why it felt right to step outside and listen.

That's why you smiled.

That's why you cried.

And that's why we rang the bells last night in Seminole Heights.

My Last Christmas

Trai Donaldson was arrested on Tuesday, November 28, 2017. The following Sunday, December 3, was the first Sunday of Advent, when we were planning to hold our annual Christmas Tree Lighting in front of the church. I wasn't sure what kind of crowd we'd get for it, but assumed considerably less than the usual 200 people or so. We'd gotten the awesome chorus of about 60 students from Jenna's high school, Blake, which is a magnet school for the arts, to come and lead some Christmas carols for us. When I invited them, I did it because they're amazing; but also because I hoped that the presence of the kids and their families might balance out the smaller size of the crowd I expected due to the murders.

With the news of the arrest, the tree lighting ended up being one of the biggest and best things that happened in my five years there. We had well over 300 people, with blankets and chairs tucked in everywhere there was space. As our choir and the Blake chorus led, hundreds of voices from our neighborhood came together to sing, finally able to sit together under the night sky without fear. It was as if they'd been set free after a long imprisonment, with those 300 people sounding more like a thousand, and afterward lingering together long into the night, just because they could.

When the event ended and the hangout began, I sat up on the side of the front steps, leaning against the porch wall, once again giving thanks for the opportunity for Seminole Heights United

Methodist to be the neighbors our neighbors needed us to be, and for giving us another moment when so many felt right at home on our campus, whether they were members, guests, or total strangers to the church.

I didn't know it at the time, but that would be my last Christmas at Seminole Heights. I would soon get the news that I would be needed elsewhere, moving to a new church the next summer. Looking back, I'm thankful to have that lingering memory—the feeling of the Holy Spirit powerfully present with us as my family, my church family, and my neighborhood family sang and laughed and lingered together. It's an image I keep stored in my soul, warming my heart with a glimpse of what is possible when a church of Jesus Christ becomes a good neighbor.

CPSIA information can be obtained
at www.ICGtesting.com
Printed in the USA
LVHW011350230721
693510LV00015B/1250